Published and distributed in
Hong Kong by CyDot Communications
Management and Technology Ltd.
www.cydot.com
E-mail: enquiry@cydot.com

Colour separation by Evergreen Colour
Separation (Scanning) Co. Ltd.

Printed and bound by C & C Offset
Printing Co. Ltd.

Designed by the author

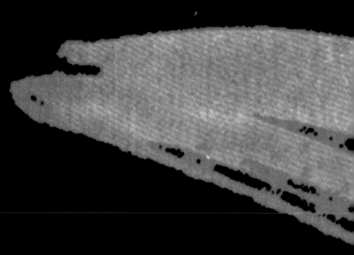

CyDot

The Dawn of a Ne
Desig

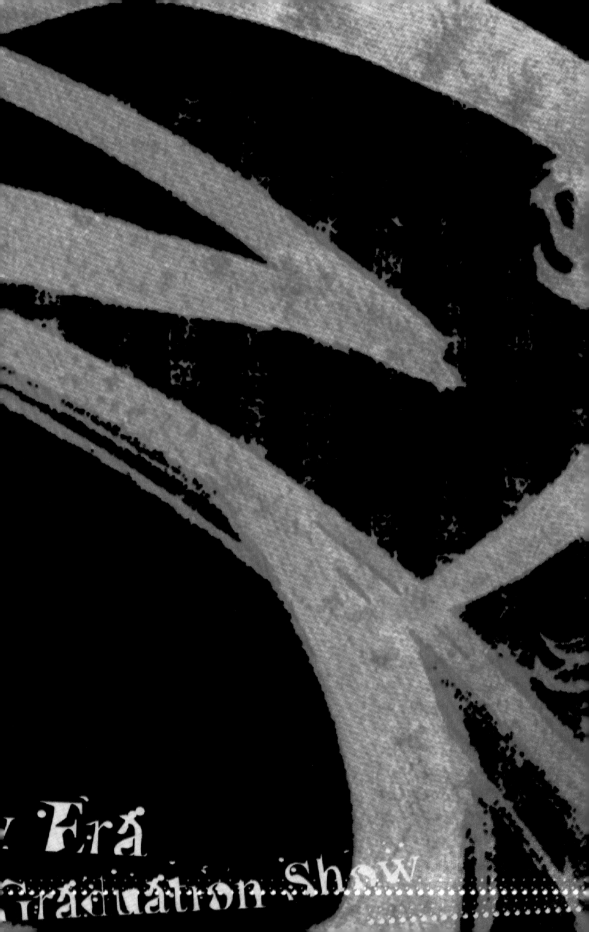

y Era

Graduation Show

A CyDot Publication

Sights of Design is a series of publications written by experienced designers or cultural practitioners, who grasp the traces of design in modern societies with internal knowledge, also from the view of spectators to evaluate and discuss design phenomenon, their impact on the cultural environment and on the people who are inside the spectrum.

What after the sights are unveiled? **Sights of Design** hopes to provoke fellow designers, even general readers, to think further about the design culture in which we are bound to work and to live, perhaps to reorient our position in society and in the economy.

Sights of Design starts with the contribution of some alumni of the MA in Design course in the School of Design, at Hong Kong Polytechnic University.

SUBJECTIVE IDeNTITY

主

經

驗

Disoriented Visual Objects

their
Creators and Users

Magdy Ma

Still, my immense gratitude to Clive Dilnot

Special thanks to Dr Hazel Clark, Bob Howlett,
Norman de Brackinghe, Tony Sin, Prof. Michael
Erlhoff and his wife, Prof. John Heskett, Alice Lan,
Dora Chu, Jeffrey Au, Anthony Chu, Landor
Associates, my colleagues and the management of
the Information Services Department, for their
comments, help and support.

This project is supported by
the Hong Kong Arts Development Council

HONG KONG A R T S
DEVELOPMENT COUNCIL
香 港 藝 術 發 展 局

The judgement and opinions expressed and the
content included in this publication do not carry
technical endorsement or authentication by, nor
necessarily represent the views of, the Hong Kong
Arts Development Council.

For my family

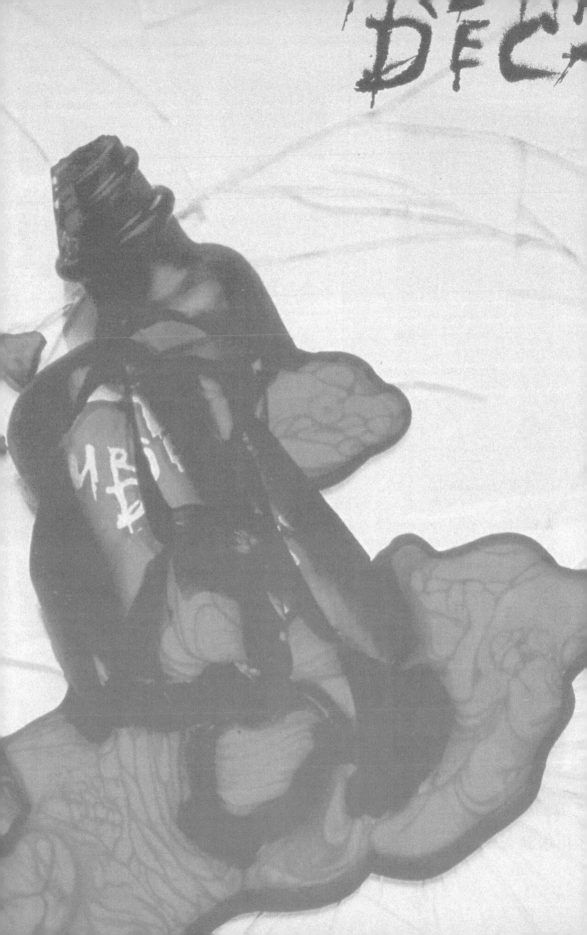

Foreword

– Norman de Brackinghe

There are not many working designers who attempt to place Design in context with society as they see it. Even fewer attempt to put their theories into words. This is made even more difficult in Hong Kong where the entrepreneurial spirit is the driving force behind the way we live. Act first and think through later!

Magdy Ma has taken on this task and whether you agree with her ideas or not she has produced a cogent argument for further research in this field. It takes courage to do that and she has thrown down the gauntlet. I hope somebody will take up the challenge and we get a serious dialogue started on the future of Design. This was a fascinating manuscript to read. As she peeled away the layers I found myself trapped in my own sophistication. Perhaps we all are? Thank you Magdy for opening the curtain on the reality of Design in Hong Kong and putting it in a historical perspective.

We want to be centre stage in the development of Innovation and Technology in the region and this is a timely reminder that it does need an intellectual rationale on which to build. Understanding our own Society is half the battle and this book is a confident step in that direction.

(Norman de Brackinghe has been working in Publishing and Graphic Arts since 1976 when he arrived in Hong Kong as a Director of Reed International. He was the founder Chairman of the Chartered Society of Designers in Hong Kong. Now retired he is still heavily involved in promoting all aspects of Design.)

Foreword

— Tony Sin

It was Sir Winston Churchill, who once said, 'We shape our building: Thereafter they shape us'.

In Magdy Ma's book *Disoriented Visual Objects, their Creators and Users,* Magdy has made some keen observations that in the long development process of Hong Kong as an international city, their *creators* and *users* have haphazardly shaped an environment that has become visually quite disorienting to the viewers – 'a fragmented visual world'. For those who grew up in this environment, they may not even aware of this phenomenon.

Magdy studied the phenomenon systematically and has identified various forces that have shaped this visual culture. Some of these influencing factors include the facts that the multitude of 'designed visual objects' lack 'communication mindfulness'; that the creators and users have an undeveloped sense of cultural identity, that they are insensitive to design value and aesthetic value of what they produce. They all function within a particular trading economy.

For the way forward Magdy stressed the importance of reorienting our design attitude from a human perspective, and rethinking our relationship with design technology to create 'a habitable visual world'.

(Mr Tony Sin studied industrial design at the Institute of Design, Illinois Institute of Technology and received his master degree from the College of Human Ecology, Cornell University. Mr Sin had worked as an interactive exhibit designer at the Ontario

Science Centre in Canada and had created many blockbuster exhibitions including China: 7,000 Years of Discovery, An Artist as A Young Machine, Soviet Spaceships and Body in Action.

Mr Sin was the founding curator of the Hong Kong Science Museum, Design and Business Development Consultant to the Gold Peak Group, Head of Design of the Hong Kong Trade Development Council, Executive Director of Pico Hong Kong Ltd. and is currently the Executive Director of Strategic Design Centre.

Mr Sin is the Director of Hong Kong Intellectual Property Society, external examiner of the School of Design, Hong Kong Polytechnic University, advisor to the School of Communication, Baptist University and China Industrial Design Association and Fellow of the Chartered Society of Designers.)

Foreword

Designer in the Age of Flexible Economy

– Peter Wing-kai Lok

To be an ethical designer today is to be a proactive designer. Proactive designer has his/her autonomous role and cultural agenda so that he/she can actively, creatively and considerately design a product, which can serve the consumer appropriately and create a 'healthy semiotic ecology'. He/She not only considers the aesthetic component embedded in the product, but also aware of the ethical consequence brought by the product. Simply speaking, he/she is very conscious of his/her role and the cultural context in which he/she works.

Unfortunately, many designers today, lacking any intellectual awareness to the cultural context surrounding them, are merely reactive designers or technocrats, who only react passively to the mechanism of what David Harvey calls the 'flexible accumulation production system'.[1] This production system emphasizes quick turnover time, with the exploration of highly specialized and small-scale market niches. However, accelerating turnover time in production would be useless unless the turnover time in consumption could also be reduced; flexible accumulation thus has been accompanied on the consumption side by paying much attention to quick-changing fashions and the mobilization of all the artifacts of need inducement and cultural transformation. David Harvey thus argues that the popular postmodern aesthetics that celebrates difference, ephemerality, spectacle, fashion, and the commodification of cultural forms, which is now disseminating in our consuming market caused directly by such 'production logic'.[2]

Therefore, the role of designer has been changed drastically in the age of flexible economy. Today, their function is to accelerate the 'death rate' of a product in order to 'give birth' to another new product or the same product with different meaning. As Jean Baudrillard says product cannot be a product without meaning today.[3] Paradoxically, product could not be a profit-making product with a stable meaning. Thus, the task of a designer is to carry out a kind of 'anti-meaning meaning-construction work' for a product, so as to adapt to the production logic of flexible economy. Thus, the postmodern aesthetics has become the most popular aesthetic form today because its ambiguous and confusing style could make a product distinctive immediately on one hand, and make it forgettable easily on the other hand.

Thus, the author's motive of arousing our ethical concern to our design industry in this book becomes very important. It can make us aware of the 'semiotic pollution' brought by a kitsch postmodern aesthetics and the destruction of creativity brought by the flexible economy. I believe anyone who works in the local design industry could more or less be inspired by the author's observation and insight. Furthermore, talking about 'ethic' today is always regarded as 'unethical' by some postmodernists, who have been attacking different discourses on truth, morality or other metaphysical assertion (ironically, such postmodernists never treat their attack as another kind of truth-claim with moral and metaphysical assumption). Thus, what the author suggests in this book does need courage and sincerity, and I think these virtues ought to be shared by the local designers as well.

(Peter Wing-kai Lok used to study in UK and has completed a MPhil thesis on "Chinese Nationalism and Hong Kong Identity" at the Department of Comparative Literature, University of Hong Kong. He is now a freelance editor and also writes about various cultural and philosophical issues.)

NOTES

1. David Harvey, *The Condition of Postmodernity* (Oxford: Blackwell,1989), pp. 147-156.
2. Ibid., p.156.
3. Jean Baudrillard, *The System of Objects* (London, Verso, 1996), pp. 197-205.

'Design is a matter of providing human dimensi
to technology.'

Clive Dilnot, :

'Immersing ourselves in an uncontrolled number
signs is impossible because doing so results in a n
kind of pollution caused by the confusion, loss, a
distortion of meaning,'

Ezio Manzini,

Preface

It seems to me as if in graphic design today, less important is the urge to communicate, more popular is a kind of pretentiousness which lays stress on style over content, and an emphasis on triviality that reduces the significance of graphic communication. It seems as if we have overcome technical problems but are facing ethical problems: Are life and truth adequately interpreted by the kinds of words and images we see in contemporary graphic design? Mechanically-refined images are sharp and vivid, almost flawless, but is such surface quality superfluous if it misses formal quality that leads to a meaningful context?

Graphics as such do not usually impress me. Rather their superficial aesthetics shock me emotionally and optically – I am annoyed by the visual disorders that frequently come into sight. I doubt if the current visual climate allows the possibility of establishing a Hong Kong design identity.

Perhaps I have to compromise in order to live with the trend – by exercising a certain degree of apathy towards these great varieties of visuals if I am unable to make sense of them, or to escape from seeing them. In doing so I feel pessimistic and trapped by an irony: the more so because as a practicing designer, I may have taken part in realizing this design phenomenon; as a viewer, I am unconsciously irritated, yet consciously embrace these sights of design driven by ideology.

But this is a condition of contemporary visual life. Graphic design is the instrument through which advertising messages deliver the commodity's beautiful promise to the potential consumer. It is the imposed ideology expressed through 2-dimensional presentation that sustains our belief in things we are told that brings pleasure or causes disturbance to our sense and sensibility. It seems more often that the unreality of commodity aesthetics works to blind our consciousness to understanding ourselves and the real world.

As suggested by Haug, the term 'commodity aesthetics',[1] on the one hand refers to visible 'beauty', to appearance; on the other, a 'beauty' developed in the mind of the buyer, 'a stimulation to the onlooker to arouse his desire to possess and the impulse to buy'.[2] It is in this process of stimulation that I feel the ethical function of graphics – the power to illuminate, to gratify – is lacking. This means that contemporary graphic design is not working for people at its best.

In speaking of 'ethics' I am not talking merely about 'professional ethics' or 'professional code of conduct' drawn up to safeguard either party – the designer or the client. Rather, I am referring to the ethos[3] of graphic language itself, by which I mean the norms and values adopted by design practitioners and the business community, as well as greater society, in recognition of an acceptable and sustainable visual language, one that embodies a graphical ethical function.

However, most visual communication is unlikely to build on ethical grounds but on commercial imperatives that do not endeavor to be human-oriented. Hence, while design is widely understood as a service to increase economic prosperity by which the quality of our material life may be improved, such improvement seems not reflected in our inner life. Do we truly benefit from objects we use and see everyday that are full of evidence of design?

In view of this uncertainty I set out to define, identify and analyze what I call disoriented visual objects and their affects on people's mentality.

Secondly, I want to question whether the prevalent visual communication language is beneficial to the development of Hong Kong graphic design. If not, away from such disorientation can we anticipate an ideal future of visual practice and thinking? Such an ideal – that lays emphasis on people's psychological reaction and the quest for spiritual value in design – might seem abstract but is ultimately the only basis on which a meaningful and lasting visual culture can be built. The task is difficult but not impossible.

Take architectural design as an area to exemplify the ideal. Architecture is about the manipulation of space for human use. Visual design, though incomparable to architecture in scale, complexity or utilitarian value, is also what people make use of to represent and express themselves. Both should be human-centered.

At its best architecture embodies spiritual value – when it gives people emotional contentment. Does this quality exist also in graphics? Possibly, it is just rarely asked for. While architecture is meant to last, graphic design is ephemeral, disposable, relatively despised in the society. The nature of graphics is transient but is it not too superficial to yield at this point, in terms of understanding what graphics can achieve?

I have always felt that spirituality can be achieved in graphics – when it touches the reader, gives satisfaction, leaves memory; when space, colour, form, image, text, meanings and associations are intelligently manipulated towards the emotional fulfillment of the receiver. The power of graphics is profound, yet subtle, almost invisible. Very often its impact on people is undetectable and this is one reason why human receptivity of graphics suffers from indifference by society.

By focusing on human receptivity, my views in this book may seem one-sided. But I prefer this conspicuous one-sidedness to being corporate-minded: as a necessary balance to attention on the economic value of design. In considering the focus of human value in graphic design one may look at Japanese graphics as a reference: acclaimed for their bold and innovative ways of interpretation, Japanese graphics are rooted in their own culture, and thus retain a strong cultural identity. They also show an awareness and expression of human spirit.

Ancient Chinese art also strove for a completeness of spiritual harmony but unfortunately this has not been inherited by contemporary design thinking. Today in Hong Kong, extensive graphics succeed in materialized presentation: borrowed ideas and images, computer as a quick-fix, inaccessibility to meaning as trend and fashion . . . whilst being indifferent to originality and identity-building. These are surface problems whereas the negligence of human sensibility is an underlying problem.

Owing to such inadequacy Hong Kong graphic practice has hardly been regarded as a respected profession; that the social perception of graphic design as marginal in the Hong Kong service industry comes as no surprise.[4]

Over the years I have observed instances of graphic inhumanity and insincerity in the visual environment. I can see people baffled by undesirable visual images, yet they leave their feelings unspoken. My contemporaries seem complacent about their performance now but uncertain of the way in which to move forward. For myself, I am fascinated by the enormous power of design technology but I don't want to become a technocrat; I have a love for Chinese cultural heritage and feel a need to express an indigenous sentiment through my work for the audience. Simultaneously I am confronted by the overt power of contemporary design styles.

I am not at all a design conservative. Nor am I a guard of the old system. I consider myself to be a disoriented visual communicator (and user) – I embrace the new but I don't want to be overwhelmed by the new. I believe there are practitioners who are bewildered, too, under new cultural and technological forces. Today, being intoxicated by superficial aesthetics, perhaps we should also try to organize content in more meaningful ways. This requires serious thinking about the basic goals of design – my concern urged me to assess the current scene in this attempt, by writing.

Design criticism in Hong Kong is scarce and immature. So it would not suprise me if some think the approach of this book impractical compared to other picture-based design books. However, my conviction is that an academic study of graphic design is as useful as a pictorial approach – both explore issues but with a different method from a different angle. The former may perhaps contribute to a deeper understanding of our young design history. After all we cannot just contribute to look at design, but not devote ourselves to thinking about it.

Developed from a study on Hong Kong graphic design for the MA design course at the Hong Kong Polytechnic University, this book targeted to design students, designers and teachers. It is my hope that it will also interest a broader audience conscious of graphic design, and the impact it has on our lives.

Magdy Ma, Hong Kong 1999

NOTES

1. 'Commodity aesthetics' is a power of ideology, a dominant force in the collective imagination of millions of people every day. It functions in the advertising system by using what is called communication 'ideological state apparatuses' (press, radio, TV . . .) through which to influence our mental and physical activity. W. H. Haug, *Critique of Commodity Aesthetics: Appearance, Sexuality and Advertising in Capitalist Society*, 1983.

2. Ibid.

3. In Karsten Harries's discussion about architecture, he understands 'ethical' as something more to do with 'ethos' than with what we usually mean by ethics. I share his view and have come to realize that today in Hong Kong, more than ever, our need for graphic design to have a code of values by which the society and the design community can live, is exigent. In this book I try to interpret 'ethics' in connection with the meaning of 'ethos'. Karsten Harries, *The Ethical Function of Architecture*, 1997.

4   Cf. Coopers & Lybrand, *Consultancy Study on Services Exports – Professional & Technical Services: Final Report*, 1996.

Introduction:
A Fragmented Visual World

Hong Kong graphic design is well on its way to the international stage of design – a belief generally held by the design community. Yet I see the discipline disoriented in this place, age and behavior.

A handful of high-profile Hong Kong graphic designers have managed to attain high international recognition. Their works, mostly treated with classical conventions although some are inspired by contemporary style, are primarily aimed at a limited number of big corporations and up-market clients. Moreover, international design firms based in Hong Kong usually adopt a global advertising image from abroad that does not necessarily represent the generality of Hong Kong standards. The wider design reality is: the massive practitioners are producing generic work that indicates a lost attitude towards thought, style and execution.

One sees emerging a trend of fragmented graphic treatment which produces visual chaos and ambiguity that dominates traditional standards of rules and order. Take, for example, in editorial design the rejection of grid restrictions in favor of graphic devices such as dots, lines, arrows, blips, layering and stretching type and imagery. I see that this approach, if not rationalized by anything, as a reflection of the designer's inability to discriminate and judge in the drift of cultural and technological transformation. This can be criticized as 'all form, no content' but nevertheless it is a fashionable graphic signature of the day.

An example of what this prevalent trend is getting at is provided by a cover design for *Ming Pao Weekly*, a leisure magazine. Traditionally called collage, the mix of images, text and popular icons from various sources constructs a composition of playfulness and distortion which is facilitated by computer features instead of cutting and pasting manually as in the old days. The graphic style accommodates the designer's explosion of ideas, it exemplifies how 'style replaces form, pastiche replaces both', yet the experimental approach seems justified here in regard to the theme of this special issue.

Such design forms appear on the printed page as well as in screen-based media; in up-market publications like corporate annual reports, in 'go-faster' graphics such as direct mail and product brochures. With brilliant colour and flexible type, they have lively lay-outs, are lavishly illustrated and extravagantly produced by advanced printing technology. Yet the contents are sometimes baffling and impenetrable to the reader. Trendy visual idioms like distortion, layering of visual elements and pastiche of Chinese and foreign motifs, tend to create confusion. Some imply dishonesty. Irrational bi-lingual typographic arrangement always results in illegibility while the tricky tone of addressing the audience is insincere.

Somehow it is our collective experience to pretend understanding of graphics as such. They possibly communicate something in their context; they do create a strong impact in things we see and read everyday; they refresh our visual experience. But do we not feel uneasy when they are so difficult to comprehend?

What shapes the flux of image and meaning is an ideological response to a changing cultural climate in which the function of forms, styles, and ideas is changed from pursuing persuasion to creating contradiction. Arbitrary visual beauty (embracing implicity and vagueness) manufactures novelty at the expense of comprehensibility; experimental designs prevail over humanitarian or utilitarian works.

This design ideology is influential worldwide yet in Hong Kong the phenomenon is also attributed to the inherent characteristics of traditional export-oriented design – the inclination to imitate, negligence of taste, and an indifference to image-building. Subject to our design past where copying was a convention, today we imitate in a contemporary sense – to replicate trendy design techniques (mainly Western) that encourage readers to 'construct meaning' and to 'reconsider preconception' through 'self-interpretation'.[1]

Moreover, worries over an uncertain political future,[2] social stability and the economic turmoil interfere with our logical design thinking, if it does exist. We are very confused about where to position ourselves in the political and social context. And when lines of approach are unclear, one produces 'disoriented visual objects'.

'Visual objects', in the context of this book, encompass conventional 2-dimensional objects such as posters and printed advertisements and 3-dimensional constructions such as store signs and billboards. By nature they are simply communication products that transmit a message by a visual statement in various physical forms. But they are termed visual 'object' in the context of this book to emphasize their humility and inferiority: for an 'object', or visual 'object', is seldom appreciated by the user for serving a practical purpose, nor considered a work of art even if a spiritual quality (which will be discussed later) is attained. Even so, their power must not be under-estimated – the variety of visual objects is so extensive, they all actively work to shape our perception of the world and to get our emotions going.

The work and value of a book, for example, is manifold. It is a tangible object that we not only optically read but also physically hold. It has human impact in many ways. One who owns a book has the satisfaction of possession (of the object); resonance to the content ; appreciation for the author's use of words and phrases. These are things that can be delivered through a beautifully 'designed' appearance and a nice configuration of text and pictures. It is a 'thing'[3] to the owner only when it embodies the desirable 'effect' – the comprehensible content, an 'identity' which reflects the taste of the reader and acts as an 'extension' to his bodily and sentient powers (the easy-reading type increases his capacity to access information and acquire knowledge). These are important concepts for their design implications.

In the city, large moving objects like trams run across the island and strike us with hybrid visual statements that dress their bodies. TV images are visual objects seen and heard; interactive design like internet webpage displays digital visual objects and invite the audience to be a manipulator/participant.

Multi-channel communication objects of the new era manipulate the needs and interests in our lives so aggressively that we wonder if this the very best of a visual life that we may have. This leads to the prime idea of this book: to question the status quo of Hong Kong graphic design – to challenge a dominant conception that the profession is a success which contributes much to the society; that our encounters with designed visual objects are always beneficial. My argument is that Hong Kong graphic expressions, which are modernized and at times bring the viewer uncomfortable moments, reflect the inadequacy of the designer who has a determinative role in the process of image/object production and dissemination. This observation triggered my inquiry into the psychological aspect of the audience.

The complexity of graphic design does not merely work in a mono-valent way but multi-valently. So to evaluate it we cannot purely read the surface or the 'type' and 'class' to which it belongs but also need to address its social meaning and human impact. For example, if we look at a route map in the railway station, when it clearly directs the way, it serves as a map and becomes a 'thing' to the visitor; if it misleads, it provokes a negative response and becomes the reader's enemy.

So understood, we should look at objects (in the context of this book, visual objects) 'not through a-priori categories but as "a sum of their effects," i.e. in terms of the work they achieve'. This explains why the merit of a poster cannot be simply judged by its appearance and its aesthetic projection but also by the way it is actually 'used' and the consequences on the user. Whether a design is properly 'used' is hard to define – it affects everybody differently, depending upon the context and individual background. Still, investigation is necessary when graphics come to pose ethical problems.

The trendy approach in commercial design – exaggerating surface and style over content; transmitting ideas into messages equivocal in terms of meanings – is usually assigned with business objectives. Thus, they unavoidably face an ethical dilemma, a challenge to the designer's sense of social responsibility.

Presumably, the designer should be a faithful interpreter but today those who produce graphics with irrelevant elements or disregard to human senses encounter no query. In the profit-minded advertiser's view, a design that boosts sales is good whichever strategy it adopts. On the receiver's side, as popular culture governs values and ideologies towards almost everything, he or she tends to be passive in this hustle of visual language – the designer finds it hard to determine ethical standards.

Thus, it is difficult to justify the ethical standard of a visual object in the commodity society. We must admit we are largely consuming images and signs of an artifact/visual artifact rather than its usefulness and practicability. It is our response to the increasingly popular adoption of semiological approach[4] in advertising. In this sense the ethical reflection of a designed object is overshadowed by its commercial value.

A lot of Hong Kong graphic design manifests itself somewhat like the subjects of discussion by Steven Heller, a New York-based writer on graphic design, who contrasts the contemporary 'layering of unharmonious graphic forms in a way that results in confusing messages,'[5] with the classical qualities of harmony and balance. Confusion and loss, which are nevertheless cultural products, pose communication problems in our society. Maybe this is why Missimo Vignelli advocates, 'believe, express and defend your responsibility towards society by not producing cultural trash'. Are we producing cultural trash, too, when we create graphics that fail to contribute to society?

To explore the above issues, this book is organized around questions of visual communication and their crucial implications on people: visual uncertainty; sensibility confusion; and comprehension and readability difficulties. To provide a context this book will briefly review local design history to see how practitioners have survived historical trading conditions to adapt to technology and Western culture in constructing the contemporary graphic face.

Firstly, we shall look at definitions of cultural terms and ethical concepts related to graphic communication. Secondly, we shall discuss the relationship of graphics to people. Thirdly, we shall look at the cause and consequence of the loss of humanity in contemporary communication design.

We then examine the so-called experimental design that arises in the presence of technology and the pretentiousness of the designer. Hong Kong design culture in its historical and economic context is investigated; and finally, we come to rethink visual strategies, looking into possibilities to improve graphic design from a human perspective – these are discussed mainly on a philosophical level.

I consider 'uncertainty' embodied in graphic design an externalization of a designer's conceited but unconscious desire to place himself at the centre of creation. But this act somehow exposes his confusion while the basic goal of design is lost. What the user suffers is basically the same – a disoriented state of mind when confronted by graphics that challenge his visual and sentient limits.

Chapter 4 reports on computer intervention in Hong Kong graphic practice and its consequences. The twin evils of 'inhumanity' and 'insincerity' in contemporary graphics also are borne of Hong Kong designers' 'copy-cat' mentality. Chapter 5 examines the traditional 'imitation'/'adaptation' – a design model first developed in a repressive export-oriented trading economy in the 19th century. My thoughts on 'an habitable visual language' in the last chapter are not intended solutions to remedy problems, they are just conceptual measures based on ethical principles hoping to deal with a practical situation. In other words, old attitudes that might be useful in new design structures.

One may notice that discussions here are not totally localized and are applicable to design elsewhere. Except for the historical and trading conditions unique to Hong Kong, most of the issues raised are so universal that they should not therefore be tied to a particular culture. My research and study has been based on a world view of design communication, whilst emphasizing the Hong Kong-style manifestations.

Western theoretical reviews are quoted to substantiate my viewpoint as local commentaries and critiques on design issues are so scarce that I can hardly draw any reference from them. To illustrate the study, visual materials are used to complement textual analysis yet examples presented here are not necessarily representational.

My concern with this neglected subject initially grew out of my own visual experience and anxiety over Hong Kong's way of design thinking. It became stronger as my observation of people's encounters with peculiar/displeasing visuals, developed. But my intention of exploring this issue is not just critical, it is based largely on the belief that people should be treated well, not only physically in contact with tangible industrial products, but also sensorily and spiritually in contact with communication products. Inquiry into the human senses is based on the presumption that good design builds on a strong basis of understanding human behavior.

I believe graphic design is an art of purpose, that the designer is a 'public' artist who owes the public a great deal. As Richard Wild (1996) points out, 'The painter's end-product, if badly conceived, will affect hardly anyone. The designer's end-product, if badly conceived, can visually or physically disrupt the lives of many people'.

This study might appear opinionated in the ways that it denigrates a great deal of design representation even though they do not pose visible harm to the audience. To some extent this is true – I want to question that which threatens us but which seems unnoticed.

To partially side-step much higher professional designs to focus largely on relatively collective (or low-end) work is the characteristic of this book. I consider generic graphics relate to the mass audience visual experience and that their ubiquity, style and language confirm their significant position in establishing a larger part of Hong Kong culture. Some up-market works are used to demonstrate their healthy approach and their positive relationship to people but these few successful works are not the subject of my discussions.

It also sounds too theoretical to recommend philosophical concepts and intellectual thinking as a means to ease design undesirabilities. This is also true: graphic problems cannot be resolved purely by abstract theorizing. However, while offering operational suggestions might look practical they take the risk of trivializing the issues – as this is already part of the problem in Hong Kong graphic design.

In any case it is not my intent, nor my capacity, to confront and remedy problems except on a philosophical level. Moreover, as there is a serious lack of critical research and analysis on local design, this critique is worth attempting as somewhat of a 'first'. I see the capacity to integrate operational knowledge with intellectual criticism of design a new responsibility for contemporary visual communicators.

As Jan Van Toorn writes, 'Valid critical judgement is the fruit not of spiritual dissociation but of an energetic collusion with everyday life' (1992), while Paul Rand, three decades ago, had agreed that 'sound and serious theory is practical' (1970). Supported by such theorizing this book is written in the hope that the literary method is equally as valid and hopefully more durable, if not more inviting as visual presentation, to express a designer's view of the visual culture in which she dwells.

NOTES

1. Self-proclaimed function of postmodernist design that is characterized by its 'chopped-up, layered, and fragmented forms, often imbued with futuristic overtones'. For more about the attitude/style of 'postmodernism', 'deconstruction' and 'postmodernism' in graphic design see Lupton, *Design Writing Research: Writing on Graphic Design*, 1996, p. 3.

2. Hong Kong ceased to be a dependent territory of the United Kingdom and became a Special Administrative Region of the People's Republic of China on July 1, 1997. The Sino-British Joint Declaration – an agreement made between the two countries – ensures the continuation of the existing economic and social system, for at least 50 years. However, social responses towards the big event vary. Some worry about their freedom and human rights post-1997 while the optimists believe things are going to turn better. A growing polarity among people and uncertainty about the future has induced a short-sighted attitude among some residents.

3. The meaning, work and value of 'thing' and 'object' in the realm of design has no big difference to us until we see the hierarchy between them through such a way of interpretation: with technology, a whole world of objects (products) is made, some of them, having been devised to successfully observe our sentient needs, to facilitate our bodily function – I believe this is what 'things' do.

To understand this we have to forget the usual meaning given to the word 'thing' either of material or of spiritual as stated in the dictionary because it can be re-interpreted as something very useful (by its implication) for visual design.

In modern commodity societies designed objects/products/artifacts are made and assigned with functions they are expected to perform. Like a directional sign, it is a visual object designed on the presumption to direct, to inform, to instruct. At times it fails to do so because as an object made for representation in the trendy world, its character may be limited to standardized beauty and utility without the embodiment of spirituality, sometimes even lacking effect (the designated function), identity (what the object reflects the user) and the power to satisfy the user's desire. But with good design thinking the function of objects can be as good as that of 'gift', or of 'thing', that which establishes a positive interrelationship between the maker and the user, the 'thing' and the user.

By commodification everything in this world is turned into a commodified object, yet by personalization (in a careful design process), an object can change its character and turn into 'thing' again. The implication for design can be exemplified, for example, in the case of 'Lap Sap Chung' (p. 163), where design acts to raise the meaning of and the function of the object. Even a good signage system (p. 165), is capable of turning a banal visual object into visual 'thing' that satisfies the user's needs.

Thus graphic images, if wisely handled, are extendible forms of representing life and thoughts, no less useful than literature, architecture or art. By nature and technology, graphic design is quite an easy-configured art of representation yet its power and influence can be profound. So it is not at all irrelevant (nor impossible) that I propose this potentiality of visual 'object' to become visual 'thing'.

The concept of 'thing' in this new dimension inspires me (for its relevance to graphic design thinking) through reading a few of Heideggar's and Baudrillard's essays on the subject, which are further explained in lectures and writings by other authors.

4. Semiology is a study of signs, an analytical/descriptive method used largely in modern advertising. By semiological approach we mean that everything is turned into signs, either object or space. The configuration and organization of a sign is based on cultural context.

5. These, in Heller's sense, are what the current so-called postmodern graphics are like. His essay, 'Cult of the Ugly' provoked an on-going debate within the American design community. *Looking Closer: Critical Writings on Graphic Design*, 1994, p. 158.

1

Cultural Forces and Ethical Questions

Postmodern Sensibilities in Modern Visuals

Postmodernism, a terminology commonly used in literature, architecture and popular culture, has emerged as a key cultural concept in western countries since the end of the 1950s or the early '60s. One postmodernist notion suggests 'the waning or extinction of the hundred-year-old modern movement (or to its ideological or aesthetic repudiation)' (Jameson, 1991, 1). Reflected in new fields of art, music, novels, films, the pioneers began by pursuing self-expression through their works – by adopting a different strategy other than formal 'modernist' styles in opposition to the seemingly dominant logic of modernism.

Wouldn't the use of the term to describe vision things sound embarrassingly pretentious? From an anti-intellectual standpoint it is. But as pointed out in the last paragraph the ideas of postmodernism have come to quite suitably represent certain visual concepts and visual techniques of contemporary graphic design. Perceiving 'deconstructed' or 'postmodern' style as the violation of conventional attitudes towards the creation of design and architecture is not unfamiliar to readers who are aware of our social and cultural climate.

Postmodernism in architecture, for example, has been said to represent 'a realization and a response to the failure of modernism . . . [on the ground that in modernism] we have allowed scientific rationality and technological thinking [to overrule] our lives, our thinking, and our practices.'[1] The realm of architecture is where the traces of postmodern

aesthetic modifications are most easily visible. The current Hong Kong cityscape, for example the Central district, is now characterized by a blooming postmodern architecture like the Entertainment Building, perhaps inspired by Michael Graves's Humana Building in New York. Century Square in D'Aguilar Street is somewhat like the American AT&T Corporate Headquarters. They are familiar modernist concrete blocks with architectural ornamentation of past style – the rejection of orthodox modernist purity in favor of decoration and ornamentation. They are refreshing visual break from the unornamented cold 'curtain wall' structures, like the Worldwide Building, that used to saturate the financial district, and still do.

Graphic postmodernism, like architectural postmodernism, is visible. They equally claim to free us from the formal limits and disadvantages of modernism. Within the design environment of the 80s, postmodernism 'has come to apply to a distinctive international style based not on dogma but on the somewhat haphazard confluence of various theories and practices of individual designers worldwide.' (Heller, 1988, 221)

Likewise in Hong Kong, postmodern culture does not refer to a systematic design style nor method. The term is used less frequently and precisely in the design field than in other arts and cultural streams, yet postmodern-like graphic design is not uncommon, rather it is prevalent in local practice. Typical ways of interpretation are blending style with new features enabled by computer technology; using multiple layered and fragmented type and images with frequent reference to foreign/historical motifs, ultimately to achieve a decorative commercially acceptable look.

Postmodern aesthetics can be found in a variety of consumer product packaging. In 'The Optical Centre' carrier bag (p. 40), visual elements are wholly replicated from Western culture – a playful combination of Charlie Chaplin's film clipping, Renaissance sculptures . . . Their meanings are detached from the original context; their forms and styles strategically manipulated in a new visual configuration. The imagery has a special foreign accent, which is attractive while presented in the local context. These visual objects are posted within our sight, their historical relevance is distant and sounds irrelevant. Looking at it our interest in searching the real meaning is diminished when somehow, a 'superficial charm' supersedes our anxiety.

The imitation of past styles, typical of postmodern image production, as Jameson puts it, comes with 'the collapse of the high-modernist ideology of style [which is unique and unmistakable] . . . and the producers of culture have nowhere to turn but to the past' (1991, 18).

Another postmodern notion suggests that the power of mass media images and popular cultural signs dominate our sense of reality, ways we define ourselves and the world around us. According to Jameson, postmodernism is not purely a style but 'a cultural dominant: a conception which allows for the presence and coexistence of a range of very different, yet subordinates, features' (1991,18).

It is also the culture of the 'simulacrum' under which 'the very memory of use value is effaced', and 'the image has become the final form of commodity reification'.[2] In Hong Kong advertising design, visual techniques/style with which the message is deliberately presented in obscure or fragmented composition can be associated with such 'cultural dominant'. As consumers we always experience a state where user value is unidentified, the emphasis on the image as the commodity is obvious. It is the beginning of the user's experience which is deliberately designed to challenge his taste, his judgement. His reaction to an ad, for example seem to reflect his such qualities.

In a magazine ad for 'Urban Decay' cosmetics (right), visual images like shattered glass, spilled nail-polish are employed in construction of an unusual visual effect. As image is a pervasive form of communication tool, when it is arranged in a surprising manner the message is more powerful because it succeeds to 'lay claim for public memory' – a function of 'picturization'.[3]

The tone of addressing the audience is somewhat like the 'deconstructive'[4] approach in cultural intellectual terms. Visual content, even the brand name, is disseminating a sense of rebel – a tone that is superficial, obscure, subversive yet enchanting. Owing to seemingly irrelevant visual impact, it creates an openness of meaning which perhaps can be incorporated into 'a romantic theory of self-expression where signification is not fixed, designers and readers share in the creation of meaning' as identified by Lupton (1996, 9).

URBAN DECAY

現在，同時選購 Urban Decay 唇膏一枝及甲油一瓶，

即可獲贈 Urban Decay 唇彩一枝。

此項優惠每位顧客只限享用一次；贈品數量有限，送完即止。

Exclusively at: *The New Face by Sogo*   HONG KONG SEIBU

Implicity is a popular approach in today's promotional culture. Graphic representation in this ad challenges aesthetic concept in conventional cosmetic promotion. As stated in their product literature: 'The alternative to the predictable palette of traditional color cosmetics . . .'

The ad delivers very little substantial information about the product but a 'commodity aesthetics' that gradually will develop in the mind of user. By providing an 'ideological happiness' 'Urban Decay' appeals to a youth subculture group who embrace the brand as a stylization of their everyday life.

The ad is designed to impress rather than just to hard sell products. It embodies the essence of postmodernism – 'intentionally conflicted and contradictory' by developing a mystification about 'beauty'. In fact postmodern transformation in graphic design does not happen incidentally but intentionally. It is 'the creation of a new constellation of cultural values, approaches and sensibilities projected in reaction to, and in opposition to the "exhausted' values of modernism'. And by 'the consciously felt exhaustion or inappropriateness of the modernist project and the range of its aesthetic criteria . . . to create new strategies of visual representation' (Dilnot, 1989).

Unconventional visual effect is a common practice and purpose in advertising by which to recognize the changing appetite of the contemporary consumer. It also reflects the felt needs of designer who finds the classical method inadequate to respond to social and cultural changes, nor to psychological condition of the creator and the user. (After all, using pretty girls, pretty faces to sell cosmetics might seem too boring an strategy in today's complex mode of life).

Lupton also observes the characteristics of post-structuralist graphic design in 'yielding a critique rather than a celebration of humanist notions of taste and originality. . . invention and revolution result from tactical aggressions against the grid' (1993, 9). I see their features – shallowness, deception . . . constructing ambiguity, failing to convey information – is offensive to people. It is from this very point – the humanistic aspect – that implications of postmodern attitude on graphic design is included in this book.

One may at first sight pay respect to the vivid visual effect yet be frustrated when one fails to grasp the ultimate meaning. In this scenario, postmodern graphics face a problem: what is appealing is on the surface, while the intended message may remain hidden. The work tends to lose a possible value and durability that good graphics may attain. However, conformity to postmodernism is inextricable in the sense that it signals a cultural and economical evolution worldwide. But the way postmodern image and representation work on people psychologically – where they pose ethical problems – is an issue worthy of scrutiny.

The Ethical Dilemma of Graphic Designers

Zygmunt Bauman points out that the postmodern approach to morality is too often described as 'the celebration of the "demise of the ethical", . . . and of the "ultimate emancipation" that follows. Ethics itself is denigrated or derided as one of the typical modern constraints now broken and destined for the dustbin of history' (1993, 2). He quotes Lipovetsky, a postmodern theorist who reinforces the above statement: 'our conduct has been freed from the last vestiges of oppressive "infinite duties", "commandments" and "absolute obligations"' (1993, 2).

Bauman asserts that if Lipovetsky is right then we are facing today a social intercourse de-coupled from obligation and duty. In fact he sees postmodernism only as 'the tearing off of the mask of illusions' that once dominated the mechanism of modernity in a negative manner (1993, 3). One must realize that Bauman advocates the acceptance of postmodernism not in the abandoning of modern moral concern but in rejection of the typically obsolete way of going about its moral problems.

When this idea is applied to visual communication I adopt Bauman's view towards postmodernism in the sense that the designer should retain moralistic visual concern but discard the over-conservative visual treatment of modernist graphic style. Undoubtedly some modernist classical rules resemble 'infinite duties' and 'commandments', but if taken as 'rules of ethics' to monitor a visual language, to maintain a balance in design, their existence could well be justified.

Far back in Western design history, the modernist role has been of significance, Steven Heller writes: 'During the late 1940s and 1950s the modernist mission was to develop design systems that would protect the global (not just corporate) visual environment from blight' (1995, 157).

It is not impossible that the essence of modernism may integrate with that of postmodernism to devise new strategies for shaping a 'habitable' design culture. The latest design and typography of Kan Tai-keung, one of Hong Kong's earliest modernist designer, are acclaimed 'pleasant and clear . . void of any strong American, Japanese or Hong Kong influence . . a sense of 'New Asia' can be felt in his work' (Idea, 1993). His notable works, having adapted to changes in conditions and circumstances of the postmodern age, a synthesis of artistic insight and skill, innovative style, grid and order of the past. They accomplish functionality and humanity as well as aesthetics to which the contemporary consumers is able to resonate.

Unfortunately, the postmodern implications on local design are more often negative: Many designers side-step the positive application and inspiration of postmodern thinking to appropriate the idea of 'free will' derived from the theory. Some indulge in breaking classical rules of visual design: constructing forms with no essential meanings. Others become lax in their professional ethics: disregarding human sensibility and social responsibility. Many emphasize a random manipulation of decorative visual gadgets, borrowed imagery from any culture of any period, that are totally incoherent.[5]

Design disorientation is also a self-reflexive process of the impact of politics on the designers. Hong Kong, having undergone its political transition, 5 is adapting itself to an upcoming social transformation. While political changes imply uncertainty of the future, they entail also a metamorphosis of belief and preference among people. Design manifestation as a mirror of social ideology tells us that the concept of values, meanings, ethics of Hong Kong people fluctuate. The designers, by means of graphic representation are reflecting their anxieties as well as that of other people in their work. One sees from the diversity of chaotic visual arrangement and indefinite visual message the wish to escape from reality and responsibility – designer's ethics are in a dilemma.

Redefining Design Ethics

To deal with this contradiction of design attitudes, we need a value system to read and to analyze their relevance so as to fairly discuss the contemporary mode of addressing the audience by graphic design. Rather than from an aesthetic perspective, this study sets out to examine contemporary graphics from an ethical view; to concentrate on their impact on the user's mental process rather than on their marketing value. That is to say, the influence of graphic design will be perceived more as a humanistic problem, less a design problem.

Frascara identifies the importance of human dimensions in graphic design: 'In visual communication, the problems are not problems of visual communication, but of people . . .' (1995, 34). How 'complicated' visual objects are literally affecting the 'complex' mind of people is nevertheless hardly controllable, and for a design to fully satisfy all people's needs is impossible because meaning changes according to context. But to achieve an average humanistic quality is the minimum the designer could achieve bearing in mind an ethical concept.

Since the user is the destination of all communication, the meaning of the term 'ethics' used here is not restricted to a moral choice between right or wrong behavior, but the benefit of him. As Sahakian suggests, it must 'deal with the good life . . . the life worth living, the life that is satisfying . . . the right act can easily be known once the greatest good has been determined, for it becomes simply that act which enhances the realization of the greatest good' (1996, 31). The ethical function invoked in this book of graphic design therefore covers two levels of reflection: the right action (in design practice/design thinking) and the accomplishment of life's greatest good (for the reader by design).

One could see how the idea practically relates to graphic communication: in creating visual materials the act of moral decision (formulation of design ideas) as a basis on which designer's ethics (the care for individual and the concern for social betterment) is projected in order to bring good life to the reader or audience, is idealistic. Conversely, the ubiquity and proliferation of mysterious graphics set out to transform human cognition into reception of peculiar ways of translating ideas, is undesirable.

The word 'ethics' throughout the book refers not only to the moral principles and philosophy governing the designing, producing, delivering and receiving of visual messages, but also an ethos (the spirit and belief in this standard) to be shared by all involving parties (the clients, the creators, and the users).

Moreover, a deeper thought regarding design ethics is derived from Manzini's advocation of 'production culture'[6] where an ethic of doing is contended. It refers to the principles of 'responsibility and solidarity that are directed toward not only present generations but towards future ones' (1992, 234). He emphasizes the importance of a general attitude such as to build the artificial environment for today and tomorrow. This, however, draw us to the visual environment of Hong Kong which definitely needs a vision for the future – to establish and conserve a visual legacy for all generations after ours.

Clearly ethical design does not merely refer to the rigid simplicity, clarity of form that unimaginatively reflect the content, but some unquantified substance that benefits the senses of the audience and the harmony within the human society.

Then what are the abstract attributes and qualities of visual objects that may possibly benefit the reader? Any ideas, techniques, methods, visuals and meanings that are infused with 'communication mindfulness', a concern for people's interpretive and optical effectiveness, an ultimate goal of design activities. However, as economies become more tuned to information-oriented and service-oriented, in design there is no problem of simple communication provided by technical equipment and technology, but whether it 'communes' with the receiver is contentious. And if it doesn't, people suffer, though inconspicuously and silently, from living a visual life where they experience moments of disorientation.

NOTES

1. Karsten Harries, *The Ethical Function of Architecture*, 1997, p. 7.

2. Baudrillard cited in Featherstone, 1991.

3. Picturization' – a phenomenon within American public culture that image is used as the most common form of public address. A primary way that ideas are packaged to instruct public conduct, which might bypass critical reason for shaping human behavior. Ideas from Stuart Ewen in his article 'Absolute Doublethink', *'And Justice for All'*, 1992. I see a similar situation in local advertising that the adoption of images (from cartoon characters, popular idols, to surrealistic pictures by technical simulations . . .) is widespread while literary references are comparatively used less.

4. A theory of deconstruction: the limits of abstract visual communication are tested by finding how many levels of meaning can be expressed through complex typographic/graphic configurations. Steven Heller & Seymour Chwast, *Graphic Design Styles*, 1988, p. 221.

5. See note. 2 in Introduction chapter.

6. In 'production culture' one passes from a 'culture of doing as production' to one of 'doing as reproduction'. Ezio Manzini, 'Prometheus of the everyday', *Discovering Design*, 1992, p. 235. With regard to graphic design I am convinced of the need for a visual culture like that of production culture which permits continuation of the existence of things.

2

Moments of Uneasiness in the Interaction
of People and Graphics

When Communication Mindfulness is Absent

What constitutes moments of uneasiness in people is the absence of communication mindfulness in undesirable graphics they deal with. Communication mindfulness, the attributes of 'detectability, discriminability, attractiveness, understandability and convincingness', are the basic performance-related concerns of visual artifacts, the axioms of design practice that form our professional manifesto. In Hong Kong's historically export-oriented economy in which the value of goods are determined by their trading value, hardly anybody worried about design mindfulness. In our modern commodity society, people become more apparent subjects of design activities in the capitalist advertising system: we are increasingly confronted by a large amount of complex signs and images that intrigue to affect our behavior.

In Papanek's sense the only thing important about design is how it relates to people;[1] Paul Rand states that graphic design in the end deals with the spectators (1995, 13). Both assertions confirm people as the target of a universe of graphic presentations. It is only when mindfulness for the receiver is achieved can that particular communication be validated for the fact that graphic deficiency poses itself as a threat to human sense to certain extent.

Graphics work to irritate our emotion and senses, when they function negatively, people are exploited, in this course of 'communication', with respect to the bodily and sentient condition at two levels – sensory and psychologically – with implications of, first, 'comprehension and readability difficulty' and second, 'offended/irritated emotion' which include also a third category, 'sensibility confusion'.

'Comprehension and readability difficulty' – a sensory reaction to obscure and illegible graphic design. Illegibility, as well as readability, is the least complex state of design failure which can be easily overcome given the awareness of the designer and user is raised. Donald Norman states the importance of having everyday things of our life designed with understandability and usability – to make things visible in office and household appliances such as user instructions (1990, 17).

Such criteria are indispensible in informational graphics, but they are not inappropriate for commercial graphics – there is no reason why TV commercials, magazines and advertisements cannot incorporate clarity and comprehensibility, simultaneously maintaining a fascinating appealing look. This is the essence of humanistic design thinking – to embody functional qualities as well as play and humor, balance and harmony to achieve a contemporary feel with a solidity of meaning.

In relation to the question of comprehensibility and readability, the distinction between 'design model'[2] and 'user's model' is sometimes ignored. To take a specific example, the integration of tunnel symbol and lettering (p. 61) fails to let some drivers efficiently access the meaning of the traffic sign because this 'design model' tends to become an isolated visual object with no 'nearness' to the potential user. Such failures can be avoided if mindfulness for the reader can be observed – for example revising the design to a 'user's model', one that drivers can react to promptly.

'Offended/irritated emotion' – the psychological rejection of unpleasant/weird/uglified graphics. Given everybody is likely to be provoked by visuals opposing personal taste or preference, the state of unease mentioned here is theorized on the grounds of a breaking of general aesthetic standards and legibility. They exist in the multitude of unthought designed visual objects that bombard us every day – those with wired layout, colliding text and picture, patches of color that suggest no meaning.

We may become emotionally irritated; we may feel offended seeing words and pictures that depict indecent meanings or feature cruelty, obscenity or violence. But the encounter is inescapable in our social context

– they are characteristics of popular gossip magazine and tabloid.

'Sensibility confusion' is unlike 'offended/irritated emotion' that takes place instantly when the viewer is provoked. It is the chaotic mental state of the viewer whose sentient capacity undergoes an ideological disturbance/dilemma when challenged by indeterminate image and its enigmatic meaning.

Sensibility confusion happens when the translation of meaning is difficult, even if the design functions to draw attention making people become the buyers. The relevance of 'sensibility confusion' is crucial – it has an inconspicuous power to overturn one's prevalent beliefs. While we used to look for beautified things in a cosmetic advertisement, we wonder why they are missing here yet we tend to be intoxicated by the new aesthetics. We as the 'addicted buyers' are simply hit by commodity aesthetics where meaning is always indefinite.

Visual Encounters of Uncertainty

'Structuralism . . . says meaning is found in the structure of the words in a sentence. Receptionism . . . says meaning ultimately exists in the value system and context of the receiver'.[3] Both sayings are substantial as well as debatable when one looks at the contemporary graphic expressions which encompass the use of words and images – their meaning is sometimes effectively delivered but very often mysteriously puzzles the receiver and creates uncertainty.

Uncertainty (or confusion), as defined earlier, causes a chaotic state of mind in the receiver when communication mindfulness is absent from a design. Visual uncertainty always refers to illegibility of visual elements whereas mental uncertainty is the confusion of meaning found in visual messages we come across everyday – in youth-oriented magazines, music packaging, TV commercials, mass-market print ads – where meanings do not necessarily adhere to their appearance but are claimed to be left for 'self-interpretation', it is when uncertainty is yet to be decoded.

But visual encounter of uncertainty poses immediate consequences if it occurs in information design like environmental graphics and directional signage. Such serious communicational media should definitely incorporate functional, readable and aesthetic visual elements for it is meant for practical use. Thus the existence of dysfunctional public transport signage that creates uncertainty is undesirable.

A transport signage is used as an example to show how uncertainty in information transmission may put the user into a dangerous state. It is the time when a sense of inhumanity and insincerity projected by the design work is felt. In speaking about disorientation brought about by graphic design I seem to refer to something abstract in fact I am trying to address myself to the actualities of visual experience in Hong Kong – and specifically, in terms of the incident from which the idea of book first arose – a circumstance of being confused/misled by an ambiguously-delivered traffic sign.

Driving on the Eastern Corridor,[4] I was heading for the Central Cross-harbor Tunnel to Kowloon Peninsula in March 1997. As I was about to change lane to enter the tunnel (about 50 kilometers away from the signboard hoisted over the expressway) as I used to do, I noticed an extra graphic device beside the old tunnel symbol. It disturbed my usual understanding of the traffic sign.

The ambiguous graphics confused me – it was out of my visual ability or assumption to grasp the meaning of this additional little icon all at once, even though I could guess it probably carried new road indications. Puzzled, I could not decide which lane to take, all of a sudden I fell into panic and was reluctantly forced to run into a lane just in time to avoid having a collision. Fifteen minutes later I emerged from the new Western Cross-harbor Tunnel . .

By adding a single Chinese character and an alphabet, the amended graphics are devised to signify directions to various tunnels. The problem is: the letters are relatively small, which is not visually apparent, thus provide insufficient warning at a reasonable distance. It brought me 'visual uncertainty' and 'sensibility confusion'. The unidentifiable graphic form literally created a 'comprehension and readability difficulty' that prevented me from acting correctly upon traffic instruction.

Initially I suspected my response was too personal and subjective. I also thought it might be a symptom of my physical inability to see well. Later I found that I shared with other drivers the undesirable experience of being frustrated by this unclear sign. Maybe I am confused only because it was new. As a matter of fact I have got used to understanding the tunnel signs. When it becomes habitual I can respond to these signs even subconsciously – a result also by accumulating experience upon learning from errors.

Yet it is my intention to point out that, for examples, traffic signs are not only meant for providing information but for regulating traffic flow that is dangerous when uncertainty occurs. Functionality in graphics of this type cannot be overlooked in designing despite the fact that any implicit instruction can be familiarized eventually.

But, as a designer, I also realize the difficulties in dealing with human response: the fluctuating human behavior and senses are something hard to grasp, adding complication to design. The body (or the sense of body), with its 'qualities and conditions, its idiosyncrasies and refusal to behave in predictable patterns of behavior make it the secret enemy of the product' (Dilnot, 1986). The graphic designer, in many cases, is found unable to cope with his enemy (human sense) that he comes to produce visual objects of uncertainty.

Ideological Uncertainty

Uncertainty in advertising graphics, a tool of trickery in contemporary advertising is different from that of information graphics in terms of their objectives and effects on people. The same standard could not be applied to both design areas. As discussed earlier, driving at high speed, receiving traffic information in a clear and precise manner is vital and literally a life-or-death issue. Uncertainty is definitely dangerous in such public communication media. Whereas an element of uncertainty, humor or wit could add fun to commercial advertising and graphic design.

One cannot deny that the unusual setting in the Urban Decay ad (p. 47) does create an attraction by its obscurity. It works on the reader through an ideological process – the ad is a sign where visual objects as signifiers attempt to bring out the signified, the product. Although in the course of interpretation one feels a confused sensibility. What exactly is the referent? What do these particular elements (broken glass, etc,) come to stand for in relation to the nature of cosmetics?

Such uncertainty lingers in the mind of the reader and possibly prompts her to become a buyer of the product. This is the amazing power of commodity aesthetics: the brand is popular perhaps for this unresolved question – 'a perpetual unfulfillment', as suggested by Williamson. She describes our desire for glamor and knowledge (through advertising) as a real need of ours, but something that can never be achieved and be understood (1981, 9).

Using signs (which create uncertainty) to mean something to the reader requires the co-operation of the receiver – in order to translate the uncertainty into something meaningful (to her). Thus, Williamson says that for the advertisement to succeed in turning products into signs, it must enter the space of the receiver who is not simply a receiver but a creator of meaning (1978, 41). In the interpretation process she finds her identity and ideological happiness.

Despite this, ideological uncertainty can be an attraction as well as exploitation, depending upon the context of the receiver. It may not be acceptable to some people who consider such sensibility confusion 'inhuman' and 'insincere' because uncertainty unavoidably imposes various degree of discomfort on people. Even so, in a society in which people are mostly concern about the status of things rather than the real meaning of things, they prefer to survive irritation brought by design, as an indication of their ideological inclination rather than a reflection of the inherent personality.

But the designer is not all responsible in this irritation process because the reader is not totally repressed (or manipulated) – there is a sentimental need of him. While visual strategy of Urban Decay ad (p. 47) is to hide authenticity by giving an aestheticized aura, the reader is enchanted; while the material content and context in the realty ad (pp. 80-81) can be misleading, our desire for living glamor is satisfied in the illusory realm of commodity aesthetics.

Thus we know so little about ourselves although we seem to see 'ourselves' in advertising image. The 'real' facet of life is blocked from view, sometimes we even take the 'reality' shown by advertisement more 'real' than the life we are living. There is an ideological uncertainty in this process of advertising manipulation on us.

However, as Haug points out, manipulation could be effective only if it somehow latched on the 'objective interest' of those being manipulated. What Haug refers to is the masses who are being manipulated while pursuing their interest. Thus the 'objective realities of happiness and unhappiness form the basis of manipulation' (Haug, 1983).

Yet, in the visual and ideological encounters of graphic design and advertising message the role of the receiver is dynamic: he can be an 'active receiver' (he who creates the meaning) or a 'static (passive) spectator'. It is his level of acceptance/tolerance/rejection that determines whether uncertainty is inhuman to him or not.

The Active Receiver; the Passive Spectator

We know graphic design affects our everyday life by the information it provides; but we seldom suspect how powerfully it affects our minds. As Peter Dormer puts it, 'graphic design promotes beliefs and ideologies . . . the sophistication and proliferation of technological media have made graphic design a powerful influence . . . it alters radically the mental and imaginative life of everyone . . . it also manufactures fantasies' (1995).

Graphic design is a means of ideology promotion and 'all ideology hails or interpellates concrete individuals as concrete subjects by the functioning of the category of the subject,' writes Althusser, 'Ideology acts or functions in such a precise operation – interpellation or hailing – just like an everyday example where the police hail an individual who turns around and simply becomes an addressed subject'.[5] Does this imply that the receiver is totally passive?

He is passive yet he is also active. While graphic design promotes ideology, the receiver is not simply a receiver but also the active creator of meaning to make ideology work – a reader of the Urban Decay ad has to be active in order to exchange himself with the person the ad speaks to, thus to access the enigmatic meaning. This happens on the grounds of his ideological conformity to the tone and style of graphic expression to which he has no rejection.

The relationship between visual image and the spectator can be viewed from a different angle – not ideologically but practically. John Berger describes our daily encounter with 'publicity image' (where graphic design serves as a vehicle): first he suggests that we are the active agents against text and images because we can walk away from a poster; turn over magazine page; switch off the TV, etc. He then makes a contradictory assertion, 'yet despite this. . . publicity images are continually passing us. . . we are static, they are dynamic'.[6]

When we are static we tend to be passive. Sometimes we just can't help being passive – when arbitrary and pervasive visual objects come into sight, we seem to be deprived of the right to refuse, as in the following situation:

In busy districts like Mong Kok, Yau Ma Tei and Wan Chai thousands of pedestrians are making their way to and fro the streets. City scene is characterized by a display of crudely-designed/printed posters that are stuck on any possible surface – lamppost, construction fences, blank walls of old residential buildings. First they are pasted side by side, then over one another. Traditionally old ones are replaced by new ones every Friday evening.

Although they are illegally put up, it has become an effective channel of communication within the popular culture. There are utilitarian graphics (like a continuing education recruitment poster) and shocking design (rock concert poster, for example) competing for the attention of a mixture of passers-by. Their contents vary but a lot of them feature obscene and violent movies screening in nearby cinemas. Whereas a Wan Chai night club poster speaks to the spectator in vulgar visual language.

Spectators are fascinated: some enjoy the sights; some feel offended. A tension can be sensed between such typical urban visual forms and the fast pace of street traffic. At times, female passers-by may be annoyed to see sickening pictures yet the encounter cannot be avoided for they must commute around these areas.

On the other hand, pornographic posters are attractive enough to some men who recognize themselves as the ones being addressed and that they are invited to act on the message. The ostensible meaning in the poster, which is a sign to this particular group of people, is put across effectively.

Graphics manipulate people's feeling enormously and diversely: they please us and they disrupt our sentiment; we are both active and passive. We are active only when the design means something to us. Like the man's favorable reaction to the girl poster. We are very likely become passive when we are not the subject, that means we are outside the ideology thus unable to recognize the value of the poster. This relationship of people and graphics is contradictory : the spectator can be spiritually 'static' or passive when visual images are dynamic and aggressive; or vice-versa, the spectator as the active-receiver.

The value and function of a graphic object are therefore determined by the desire, taste, knowledge and context of the receiver: Wan Chai night club posters bring fantasies to the male neighborhood, arouse their sensory and psychological curiosity; pop music concert posters function in the youth subculture; obscene movie posters disturb the female viewer. On the basis of the above observation that people are sometimes impaired in this visual experience, it is clear that design inhumanity is inescapable. What is important now is to explore the definition of inhumanity in graphic design.

NOTES

1. Victor Papanek cited in Dan Imhoff, *Communication Arts*, May/June 1998.
2. Donald Norman, *The Design of Everyday Things*, 1989, p. 17.
3. D.K.Holland, 'When Yin collides with Yang', *Design Annual, Communication Arts*, 1995.
4. Eastern Corridor is an expressway running along the coastline of Hong Kong island, from the east of Hong Kong to Central. There are plenty of exits, each of them leads to either Causeway Bay, Central District, or through the Central Cross-harbor Tunnel, Eastern Harbor Tunnel or Western Harbor to the Kowloon peninsula.
5. Louis Althusser, 'Ideology and Ideological State Apparatuses', *Mapping Ideology*, 1971, p. 110.
6. John Berger, *Ways of Seeing*, 1977, p. 130.

3

The Loss of Humanity in Communication
Design: Contemporary Symptoms

The Emergence of Inhumanity

In the context of this book undesirable graphics are termed 'inhuman' and 'insincere' to distinguish their function (or 'malfunction' would be a more appropriate word) from that of graphics endeavor to work for man, to act on the reader's expectation. The more unserviceable visual encounters take place the more harm they work on the reader – his sense of the reality eroded, his confidence lost, and the ability of discrimination and judgement may subsequently diminish.

This is always the case though not noticed by most of us. Still, using the word 'inhuman' to speak of graphic impact might seem over-exaggerated to some readers. But if we recognize people as the goal of all acts of making in the design world, we must admit the process does occasionally generate inhuman moments for people. Who never had the slightest frustration in dealing with graphic images and meaning?

I was first triggered by the concept Keith Tester offers in *The Inhuman Condition*. He argues that 'many commodities in the world leave us dissatisfied, we all try to make sense of our humanity by turning elsewhere: to inhuman things' (1995). He asserts that the making of the human world creates domains of the inhuman and it implies process of dehumanization.

My thought on this issue developed through reading Christopher Jones's *Essays in Design* where the notion of 'inhumanness by human effort' is introduced. With less abstraction, Jones describes the emergence of 'inhumanity' in the 'man-made' world. He notices at the present time, technology and the ways of living with technology seem in some profound, indefinable yet very real way inhuman, yet they are the results of human effort (1984, 31).

Jones is talking about occurrence in the field of industrial work and planning where he sees an 'obvious' inhumanity. In visual design, however, it is intangible inhumanity that is confronting us. The abstract quality is found in the surface manifestation, say by turning the otherwise clear type into illegible words. It also resides underneath in the meaning of advertising messages that cause discomfort to our mental state – they are inhuman when attraction becomes exploitation.

Tester says people are so confused by the wonders, sights and sounds that constantly make their felt presence around us. Graphic design offer us sights of wonder, truth as well as falsehood, more effectively today by computerization. In most circumstances they serve as bridges of communication but the thoughts in contemporary styles are increasingly intangible as technology becomes more accessible – has technology taken part in bringing inhumanity too?

As we have seen, the suffering of man induced by man-made objects in both the physical dimension and psychological dimension (which is inconspicuous) of people is a hindrance to our task of designing. However it is the 'inexpressibility of psychological pain' that is more problematic because it might be a sign of human intelligence in regression.

We have uneasy moments when using all kinds of objects, yet the feeling of having our senses punctured can be expressed only if it can be articulated at all. Instead of questioning there is a general tendency among people to feel somewhat enchanted by the status quo – an illusory realm in which the world is conquered with the making of all kinds of objects, in all desired forms and shapes by different modes of representation and reproduction. This self-satisfaction (or self-deception) could just paralyze oneself!

There is a similarity between the above statement and Tester's view of the commodity world. He writes, 'we live in a world which tends to be experienced precisely as enchanted . . . it is also likely to be experienced as quite natural . . . but if we do not construct our lives as somewhat natural, it is scarcely likely that our lives will hold any purpose or reason for us' (1995). Is not the human condition frustrating?

The problem of inhumanity arises from this uncontrollable condition that everything forces the individual to follow and live within. Undesirable feeling is substantiated by the ideological power of advertising, that is a condition of our social life.

That is why Seiden condemns advertising, 'some weird, mystical science by which a few control the masses. It takes advantage of little-known psychological factors plus the electronic media to sell us things we don't need and can't afford. It is a refined version of brainwashing . . .' (1988). But advertising has its economic importance despite the huge quantity of semiotic signs greatly confusing human senses.

In screen-based graphics, the problem of illegibility and incomprehensibility is inducing a condition of inhumanity that challenges the user who are also immersed in 'the overload of information provided by the media which now confront us with endless flow of fascinating images and simulations . . .'.[1] Apparently in the information age few people can totally escape from the continuous overload of information on multi media that tends to use up a lot of our time searching and browsing, at times driving our mind into guessing or 'puzzling'.[2]

In this sense it is questionable whether the World Wide Web on the internet, as a technological advance to accelerate the transmission of information through the network of computers among users, totally benefits the user or not.

A newspaper columnist expresses her Internet experience, 'I use the Internet everyday but only because I have to, and not because I think it is the all-powerful, all-liberating, all knowing road to the future or any other such nonsense . . . a lot of it is inaccurate, unreliable, irrelevant, self-indulgent, badly written and impossible to find except by accident.'[3]

Another columnist writes, 'The information age is a fascinating thing. Hi-tech is the vital tool by which misinformation is spread around the world in minutes, rather than days or weeks',[4] – a response to the phenomenon of false electronic information transmission through the internet. He considers this a moral issue that is 'pertinent to all who study the growing effects of the information age'.[5]

The faddishness and inhumanity of technology are exemplified in some Web pages – unconstrained; filled with ads; frequently littered with junk; composition of images is chaotic; information unstable. But this is not at all to denigrate what the internet has offered people – in fact some interactive design does enable functional and 'happy navigating' by users when the attitude of the interactive designer works towards the benefit of the user. Recently the site of Hong Kong Web designer Lemon was praised as 'a showcase of Web savvy.'[16] Lemon effectively takes the viewer to surf through the site by clear visual ingredients integrated with effective structural elements.

Both inhumanity and insincerity are contemporary symptoms of disoriented ethics in design but insincerity is however an inevitable ingredient of advertising that it is not usually speculated.

The Extent of Insincerity

Insincerity differs from inhumanity in that the former works basically on the viewer's sentiment while the latter effects its undesirability on people physically and mentally. 'Insincerity' seems mild and trivial compared to the ever-powerful impact of 'inhumanity', especially when one looks at it not from a human perspective, but with a commercial objective (in this sense, insincerity is almost all that advertising asks for, in order to profit in the commodity world).

Insincerity of visual objects forms an integral part of the origin of design problems discussed throughout this entire book. Before going further it might be useful to understand what I take it to mean to be sincere in graphic design.

Among modes of addressing the audience by graphic design like classical, experimental, the latter is nevertheless meant to be radical, self-centered – a kind of aesthetic exploration with (sometimes without) a designated audience. It can be personalized, idiosyncratic or even outrageous. Representation style is open as long as it is not alleged to be utilitarian or informative. Yet to bear such a name still it ought to be 'sincere' (a self-commitment) – to endeavor to what it urges us to be doing. Thus to invoke transmission of unmistakable information by 'experimental' graphics is a dangerous act.

This might seem abstract (perhaps absurd) but indeed is concrete in many instances: it is not uncommon that signage systems of certain public areas are inclined to a more stylistic graphic approach by which the rules of legibility are sometimes overlooked; haven't we ever been misled by an obscure directory and got weary in finding our way out of the enclosed artificial space of a new, large shopping mall?

To be really sincere is central in information graphics. Under this category the layout and content inevitably need to be informative, functional, thoughtful, considerate – everything to do with the user in mind. Personalization of design experiment is inappropriate in this facet of design. If ever it is done, there is a tendency to become insincere – by the nature of individualization that may easily separate people from communicating with each other.

For example in the typographic field, with type design software thousands of fonts are designed every years, anyone and everyone may freely utilize them, to construct an unique type for himself is no longer a problem. It is very likely that a lot of non-communicative solutions will come out of the easy access to this immense resource, none of us using identifiable fonts in communication design.

To be sincere, therefore, is to release the meaning of a visual object for its audience to access – not just clearly but strategically presented with wit and elegance. Maybe I should argue with less idealism but with some reservation: to maintain a most consistent possible way of being able to convey the message with the least irritation and inconvenience to the reader; at the same time to achieve a fashionable and pleasing look.

'Insincerity', on the other hand, is deceitful. It refers to the trickery and unfaithfulness embedded in the meaning of graphics, both a physical and abstract state of visual deviation in the existence of 'irresponsibility', 'exaggeration' or 'sophistication'. It reflects deviated ethics in the designer, and of the object itself through which these various types of insincerity may work singly or coincidentally on the reader.

Since many competitive commodities these days have very few differences in function and appearance, being factual and straight-forward in product/service promotion may seem insufficient to arrest the reader's attention. There is a tendency in advertising campaigns where 'aestheticization of life' is a common approach.

The blooming of Hong Kong's realty market in 1996 was extraordinary. It led to keen competition among realtors, it also benefited the advertising business in terms of the extensive sales promotion campaigns required to be launched. In a series of realty press ads, the creation of dreamland and dreamlife appear to be unnatural yet undeniably attractive to the audience. It is an aestheticization of life resulting to a hullicination of the reader, by the designer's effort with commercial imperatives.

Landscape shown on the ads has been retouched adding greenery and a luxurious spacious look. The visual complexity is enchanting despite the fact that one can feel the aura in the photograph a bit artificial. Yet virtual reality (which is always a perfect situation) is irresistible, the reader's attention is captured, a fantasy is created.

The illusory dimension is set up to satisfy people's desire for living glamor. It flatters by creating a prestigious image which the reader accepts for himself. Insincerity is generated in trying to convey a hallucination/false information about the quality of the advertised property. Or it can be said that it is just a theatrical representation of the real location.

Semiologically the reality is transformed into a sign (represented by fairy-tale perfect-looking human characters) with fragmentation of space and time (the loss of depth of environment and indefinite time of happening). This is 'hyper-reality' – the imaginary side of life.[7] It is a common advertising tactic in the simulational world where 'the real is emptied out and the contradiction between the real and imaginary is effaced'.[8]

There is nothing wrong with this approach from business perspective – in fact it is commercially successful. It is justified designwise but ethically it projects a false image of the reality – but false image is valid to garnish our everyday banal life .

The use of a sophisticated surreal view picture (false image) is a marketing strategy in the promotional culture. Within the consciousness of the consumers there is a 'worshiping of false image' (Norman, 1990, 174) that has sustained this kind of advertising tactics.

Such consumer psychological complex is not peculiar, it is a function of ideology. Potential property buyers are easily deceived by the make-believe for a while. However, satisfaction derived from the false image may depreciate when the completed homes and landscape are found less gorgeous than the artist's impression.

Hawkins points out that 'sophistication' has two meanings relevant to advertising design: (1) deprived of original simplicity . . . (2) misrepresentation in argument . . . fallacious reasoning'. The approach of 'sophistication' in design is a timeless golden rule that ensures reader awareness. The extent of it determines the degree and consequences of insincerity: at best it aesthetizes our everyday life subtly and naturally; at worst, the meaning of a design becomes deceitful.

Such ideology and advertising theories on which design is based inevitably generate insincerity – a characteristic of our design culture. Is there any limitation in people at all, to confront these forces? Indeed, our limit to dealing with the increasing mass of information is yet to be discovered, as identified by Manzini, who introduces the concept of 'semiotic pollution' to describe the condition.

Semiotic Pollution: the Production of Confusion

In Hong Kong, as in other big cities in the world, modernity has led to the diffuse production of material artifacts and immaterial advertising statements. They partially upgrade our standard of living and increase our knowledge about the world. They also impose uncomfortable moments on us. To say so is to respond to a design phenomenon, semiotic pollution, in which people are unconsciously located.

Today in the commodity society, not only has 'a world of [physical] objects without depth'[9] been produced, but also a sea of visual objects disseminating some untrue, exaggerated, mixed messages to us. It is the work of advertising. Already in 1971 Victor Papanek accused advertising design of being the phoniest profession in existence because of its nature to persuade and impress people to become consumers, to purchase what they may not need with money they don't have and to do what they might not do if not driven by advertisements.

Advertising is never a mere conveyance of factual material. But competing promotional strategies seem to push forward the emergence of a more problematic language – one that comprises superficiality, dishonesty, deception. The so-called commodity aesthetics permeates all advertising media. For example, visual form that do not bear any significant meaning, nor commitment, but subjective and ephemeral expressions.

We are in the course of making a 'world of [visual] objects without depth that leaves no trace in our memory, but does leave a growing mountain of refuse'. Within this existential condition, one sees the proliferation of 'semiotic refuse'.[10]

The flourishing advertising and publishing industries of Hong Kong accelerate the production of 'semiotic refuse'. Every day we come across a huge number of visual gadgets and visual information. News stands are saturated with news and fashion magazines, newspaper, comic books and periodicals that disseminate ideas that we cannot totally trust; the electronic media are occupied with plausible ideas from the advertisers; junk mail thrown to your door seems to enrich your choice of consumption, yet it impinges on your right of rejection as well.

Either from a design or human perspective, we need to look into this question. Because 'the multiplication and continuous transformation of forms, colors, and textures of objects can lead to the impossibility of reading any real difference and any real meaning in them . . . This difficulty in decoding the language of things is a fundamental aspect of the communication problems we are facing nowadays in the technology age' (Manzini, 1992, 241).

The material implication of advertising and printing products is problematic in a way that it manufactures physical refuse within our living environment (the biosphere). But the production of semiotic refuse in our visual environment (the semiosphere) is even harder to deal with because of its abstract existence and inconspicuous effects on people.

Manzini states this condition, '[apart from physical limits], we are in the process of discovering another limit: the limit of our capacity to deal with an increasing mass of information,' he continues, 'immersing ourselves in an uncontrolled number of signs is impossible because doing so results in a new kind of pollution: semiotic pollution, caused by the confusion, loss, and distortion of meaning . . . [is] the production of a big 'noise' which is precisely the opposite of what that increase in information meant to add' (1992, 223).

Could one escape from the big 'noise'? Could we reject the 'increasing mass of information'? Quite impossible, because signs and codes are ubiquitous and the power of 'noise' is enormous. But it should also be understood that the feeling of one person is not absolute for everybody: one may find an advertisement fascinating and entertaining, whilst another regards it offensive. Designers are meant to create user-experience by the form and meaning of designed objects, yet we have to observe user-feeling upon the user-experience.

A recent example from the local consumer market – the rigorous competition among mobile phones of different brands – provides a case illustrating semiotic pollution in the contemporary setting of Hong Kong.

With telecommunication innovation, the possession and use of mobile phone has become so common and popular in a way that the concept of cellular communication has been radically altered. Today a portable phone is not for emergency use nor urgent business discussions with people in a distant place, rather, over the phone we chat with friends just across the street, sometimes for hours, on an unimportant topic.

Advanced digital networks allow the technological function. Consumers access information on the availability of such functions and services through advertising.

To pitch for their commercial chance in the market, advertisers compete savagely for our attention by all means: big-budget TV commercials using celebrities, in the form of gigantic out-door billboards at cross-harbor tunnel entrances, product/service brochures designed with sophistication, printed in vibrant colors. Sometimes they are distributed to you by hand – you may possibly receive quite a few of them walking down a street in Causeway Bay.

It is a process of dissemination of a sense of smart-consumption to the public. We are immersed in semiotic pollution, striving to become smart consumers. In fact mobile phones of various brands look very much alike; they function more or less similarly despite differences in their transmission capacity. It is by a semiotic approach by which products are equipped with personality giving it added-value, and to manufacture associated concepts such as artistic look, executive style, or to boost their advantage as trendy accessories.

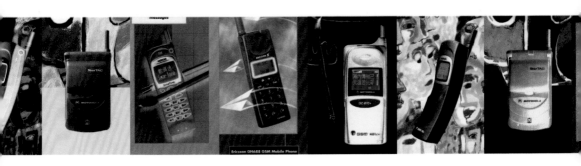

Ericsson GH688 GSM Mobile Phone

These codes and 'fetishized signs'[11] are developed to appeal to a particular consumer group to satisfy individual desires. The periodical design and redesign of the commodity appearance is to create and generate new meanings to persuade fresh consumption. An interesting argument raised by John Berger who points out the advertisers' intrigue. He states that while one brand competes with another, they also confirm and enhance each other (1992, 131).

In the advertising system the consumer seems to be placed at a high position in the advertiser-consumer relationship in such a way that he is free to take what he wants from many choices. Yet to be suspicious one can feel that the advertiser is intentionally steering the meaning of these ads to confuse our sense of discrimination. As Goldman explains, '[the advert] numbs us to the process of recombining meanings' (1992, 38). By semiotic pollution, are we provided with an 'illusion of choice',[12] a 'boredom of choice' or the 'freedom of choice'? The human impact of design and advertising seems an evasive topic among people.

The Indifference to the Human Impact of Designed Visual Objects

Visual objects and visual messages, in different forms of appearance, are affect people at different levels. As identified in the earlier sections these effects are undesirable to people to a great extent. However the varied quality (and existence) of 'inhumanness' in graphics is abstract, its relevance has never constituted an issue in our society. But if the task of graphic design is considered significant in a human society, then the proliferation of nonsensical visual objects is just as problematic as that of 'non-useless' physical objects.

With the rise of commodity production our everyday experience of using designed objects is distressful because many of them are 'uncannily disturbing to our senses of reality' (Dilnot, 1992). In fact our contact, both with industrial products (such as an uncomfortable chair), and graphic objects (like a 'hard to read, and uninviting' poster) may irritate our physicality and mentality. While an unpleasant visual encounter seems ephemeral (the life of a poster is short and our contact with it seems shorter); the chair (where either beauty or utility is missing) may frustrate you every time you sit on it. Yet the malfunction of physical objects invites more social attention. But is it all that simple that graphic failures do not affect people at all?

Contemporary visual objects are more than 2-dimensional static displays assigned with shapes and colors but also form a power instrument that touches our sentiment. Despite an underlying uncertainty of meaning and a sense of inhumanity, some feel as if the phenomenon is normal; others are obsessed by eccentric style and form, hidden meaning and the special kind of 'taste' that it seems to carry.

The question of graphic exploitation is little noticed because the invisible influence on readers is not as prominent as that from a badly-designed product. Hence, complaints like: 'being offended by an advertisement,' or 'misinformed by a road sign', are culturally regarded as trivial. How undesirable graphics disrupt the spectator's mind is treated with little enthusiasm – it is not felt destructive by the spectator himself who, after all, will soon learn to inhabit the given 'designed visual environment'.

Visual communication is meant to reach over sociology, psychology and marketing. Over time, however, it is human psychology in relation to consumption behavior that invites most investigation. Although Victor Papanek considers advertising design a profession more harmful and phonier than industrial design (1992), the subject of his discussion – graphic design – has not undergone adequate scrutiny from a human perspective.

All over the world in the design disciplines largely observe human impact with seriousness: in industrial design, ergonomics and product semantics are basic considerations; in architecture and interior design, human behavior is taken into account in the design and construction of buildings and in allocating interior space; discourse on weakly-designed products and their effects on users is raised from time to time; plenty of books give detailed examination of malfunctions of poor designs.[13]

In Hong Kong, however, there is scarcely any thought/argument/study raised on this subject. But clearly-delivered, responsible designs are well received, and taken for granted (this is fair for that is what design is meant for). Absurd graphics, hollow symbolic works are sometimes awarded as innovative creations or, when considered not praise-worthy, treated with evasion; in kitsch graphics (those embracing bad taste) a trendy cultural term is affixed (by the creator or advertiser) to legitimate its existence.

The city of Hong Kong is beautiful at a glance, especially at night when thousands of neon lights brighten the streets. Looking closer, one sees the ugliness of the juxtaposition of store signs, fabricated in a mix of synthetic material, glittering and competing along Nathan Road. Dreadful color painted on public facilities spoils the view of our parks along with interweaving and everchanging billboards erected over one another in the most expensive district of Causeway Bay and Tsim Sha Tsui.

The chaos strikes our nerve yet these are characteristics of the city: the ugliness of our street scene has been publicized as beautiful sight indigenous to Hong Kong, as described in the Tourist Association's guide to visitors. But from a design point of view it is disastrous for it reflects a lack of determination in the organization and integration of words and images for

the real user's (the inhabitant's not the tourist's) visual pleasure. As a matter of fact, we as the spectators can only behave as Crozier describes, 'people adapt to circumstances and often respond to changes in their environment with inertia. . .' (1994, 117).

Public and commercial visual objects in the city are sometimes offensive to people yet they are passive in this relationship. The designers and the co-producers who fabricate this abundance of visual distress assume the audience to take everything they produce, which indicates an ignorance of ethical concepts in their profession.

Ethical thinking is central to graphic design and should not be taken as marginal to innovative thinking. But the reality is: for the complacent designers, even if the problems are made known to them, their strategy is to remain being indifferent and intact. For the business owner who profits from the present mode of graphic representation and reproduction, the exploration of human values is superfluous.

Does this case imply that as economy and technology advance, human expectation will decline, reduced to just a compromise? The indifferent attitude seems to take the corrosive impact of design as just inevitable consequences of cultural transformation. Perhaps this is why, a stream of thought and practice, for example, in graphic design, is taking precedence over human-oriented strategies – the emergence of the so-called experimental design.

NOTES

1. Baudrillard cited in Featherstone, 1991, p. 68.
2. The way Paul Rand describes the audience's feeling towards the mass of printed material, effect of the manipulation of graphic idioms, *Design Form and Chaos*, p.119.
3. Alice Cairns, *South China Morning Post*, 1998.
4. Charles Martin, *Postmagazine*, 1998.
5. Ibid.
6. The site of Lemon design agency of Hong Kong is considered typical of good homepage design which 'intelligently play with the semiotics of online media and their technological metaphors is rare on the Web,' writes Max Bruinsma, *Eye*, 1997, p. 38.
7. Featherstone, 1991, p. 65.
8. Ibid. ,p. 69.

9. Ezio Manzini describes the making of worthless products by new technological possibilities. 'Promethus of the Everyday', *Discovering Design*, 1992, p. 222.

10. The concept of 'semiotic ecology' was proposed by Volli in 1988. It refers to a semiotic space in which messages, texts, and codes cooperate and compete at the same time. When man is condemned to live in the midst unable to reestablish them, they become semiotic wastes or semiotic refuse that pollute the visual environment. Ugo Volli, cited in Ezio Manzini, 'Promethus of the Everyday', *Discovering Design*, 1992, p. 241.

11. According to Goldman, what advertisers entwine in the ads preferred interpretation is an ideology of commodity fetishism. *Reading Ads Socially*. 1992, p. 39.

12. Judith Williams says that by 'appellation' of the audience, which is an advertising strategy, we are trapped in the very illusion of choice. *Decoding Advertising: Ideology and Meaning in Advertising*, 1981, p. 54.

13. Just to name a few books on the subject of public response to industrial design, and the moral responsibility of designers in the society – *Discovering Design, Design for the Real World, The Design of Everyday things*, etc.

4

Style-Emphasis and Technology Intervention

Experimental Design: Superficial Aesthetics of the Computer Age

Given that design style is constantly changeable, communication mindfulness is nevertheless the basic requirement (and the intrinsic property) of design. The 1990s have seen the emergence of a new aesthetics characterized by a self-indulgent visual statement with a loss of humanity. The radical graphic designer is keen on exaggerating everything by giving it an inaccessible quality: an eccentric look with enigmatic meaning which, perhaps, is a result of design disorientation in the technology age.

Robin Kinross observes the appearing of such confusion in the world of typographic and graphic design. He puts it, 'mundane reality was blocked from view . . . each person could inhabit their own bubble of meaning, something could mean anything, and so quickly it could only mean nothing'.[1] Perhaps the 'nothingness' is the message, a message with no real commitment but a reflection of the designer's pretentiousness as in 'experimental' graphics.

The term 'experimental' for example in publication design, has come to stand for brutal manipulation of image and typography, those attempt to break every conventional rule with no logic. Weird arrangements of visual elements are labeled 'experimental' – a design language strives to be 'self-expressive', 'trendy', 'subversive' and 'revolutionary'. As Rick Poynor describes the design of *Ray Gun*, an American popular music magazine, 'scribbles and photographs had been upended across the pages and stuck down where they fell . . . letters drifting so apart that you had to piece them together yourselves to make words.'

While visual experiment in editorial design is usually represented by clashing columns of text with exaggerated spacing (or negative leading), other experimental graphics may appear like a static form of presentation by print inspired by visual approach in the television environment, say, MTV (Music TV) which is always a random shifting of lights and objects with any context. They are the cliches of today that do not require any reason or aesthetic standard of any kind to justify their appropriateness.

Hong Kong graphic design is not behind in the drift. The concept is now assimilated by the design practice, among the inexperienced designers, design students and within a considerate number of professional practitioners. The way it is widely used irrespective of circumstances, needs and effects makes it a problematic issue.

In experimental approach, trendy beauty is substitution for reader-friendly beauty. They are considered avant-garde attracting admiration of followers and curiosity of layman audience. Shown here is a piece of student's work which denotes the students' aspiration by an experimentation. But the deliberate negligence to type legibility is undesirable.

Even though the text of this invitation card for a design graduation show (right) is quite illegible, it captures attention; it vaguely delivers significant information such as place, time and date but it creates an impact. The designer, a student, is heavily influenced by the current experimental design climate from the way he ignores classical rules of typography but lends himself to experience randomly-placed ragged type and forms. Frankly speaking, the infusion of Chinese sensibility (what the jumping fish depicts) to the design is wit, but the eclectic play of typography induces optical obstacle – possibly intentionally but is problematic as a communication device.

The invitation demonstrates a unconventional aesthetic approach. A pretension of young student designer whose own aesthetic need is accommodated while the reader undergoes an interpretation difficulty. By this typographical treatment, legibility is failing, however, readability exists, in the ways it promotes interest and the challenge of reading it.

According to a student who participated in the creation of the visual identity, it is their conscious attempt to experiment with this particular style by which the meaning is

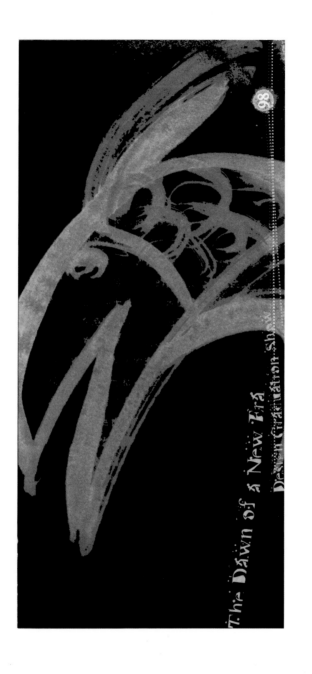

The Dawn of a New Era
Design Graduation Show

98

Guest of Honour: Mr Victor Lo Chung-Wing, Gole, Peak Treasures (Holdings) Ltd.

Opening and Award presentations: 26 June, 4pm

Hong Kong Polytechnic University
School of Design
Core A, First Floor
27 June – 30 June,
10 a.m. – 8 p.m.
1 July closes 2 p.m.
Opening 26 June 7 p.m.

BA (Hons) Fashion Design, BA (Hons) Graphic Design, BA (Hons) Industrial Design, BA (Hons) Interior Design, BA (Hons) Photographic Design, BA (Hons) Art & Design in Education, Diploma in Design, PhD Jewellery Design purposefully left to be explored and translated by the individual audience in his own way. Perhaps, this is what Robin Kinross calls, 'politics of the time: when a sense of things in common was displaced by free-for-all individualism . . .' (1996).

Does this Hong Kong student's design belong to one of the 'current plethora of aesthetically questionable graphic output' (1994, 155)? – a remark made by Steven Heller on some American design students' work. Under the powerful postmodernist influence, students from different cultures behave alike. Living in an international modern city our inherent Chinese tradition does not prevent us from taking in Western ideology, rather both cultures are synthesized enabling the birth of a hybrid culture.

Fostered by the school's policy of 'giving free vein to their creativity, without commercial restraints'[2] students' concerns lie chiefly in their self-satisfaction and the judgement of their peers, rather than the response of the business community or the general public.

Experimental design, though claimed to be 'on-campus projects' not intending to function in the real world, should nevertheless observe the objectives of graphic communication. Indeed the educational institute has provided a place, setting and freedom for students to express their intelligence, and while they are protected from having the working practitioner's responsibility for the commercial interest, doesn't the word experiment, 'come to justify a multitude of sins?' (Heller, 1994, 155)

Visually experimental works by the stressing of style, insincere tone and abandon of balance indicates an evasion from ethical concern. The incident indicates another issue: students tend to acquire little knowledge of the alternative classical typography which is fundamental in the broader application of visual communication in real practice. Perhaps students should think about how the radically new could coexist with legibility.

Out there in the real world, there is a multitude of visual artifacts tending to deform instead of inform; sometimes disregarding integrity, destroying authenticity; hiding substances or distorting meaning. This imposes disharmony in our visual experience. Are we aware of this at all? Not really, for we usually take it as natural although, somehow, we may feel a sensibility confusion.

The excessive play with pure form may be a conformity to postmodern aesthetics, a response to technocratic impulse or the intuition of a pretentious graphic designer. Apparently absurd and indistinct graphic messages take control of our senses and association; our ideological, aesthetic and ethic standard are unconsciously altered to accept what is unfolded before us. I am conceived that even if computer possibilities are accelerating the trend of experimental design it is less the problem of technology but more a problem of people (the designers) who are pretentious with an obsession with the computer features that they utilize in the job of 'designing'.

The human factor is important. By this I mean the creator, whose ethical reflection in the work, I consider, is more powerful than any other forces. To pursue the origin and consequences of experimental graphics, my focus will be placed on firstly the designer's attitude and secondly the intervention of computer technology, both of significance in bringing about this phenomenon.

Experimental Design and the Pretentious Designer

Jan van Toorn observes a phenomenon in the commodity society: the consumer has become dependent upon an increasing density of communicative networks in which the designer holds a mediating role between corporate and public interests. In his sense, the designer should renegotiate an attitude which is related to the benefit of all, but most importantly, not to falsify the reality of life.[3]

If van Toorn's view is substantial, does it mean that the best and the simplest thing a designer can do is to correctly and precisely deliver the truth? Obviously design cannot be as straight-forward as telling truth these days. Contemporary consumers want novelty and attraction, perhaps excitement – which are qualities now we call commodity aesthetics. However, as I wrote earlier, attraction may become exploitation, the over-use of gimmicks and tricks possibly challenge the limit of human senses, if not impairing them.

Even so, in the ego and arrogance of the designer, pretentiousness as attitude and style is prominent in contemporary design. According to Heideggar, man has perceived himself, in the modern period, as the subject who is able to represent the world (as object), either literally as images, in the form of codified representations (as drawings), or in other abstracted and symbolic forms. In this respect, the designer is expected to take the lead (among members of other professions in the society) to represent the world by meaningful, functional, aesthetical forms and messages, in the interests of people.

Yet the contemporary designer, who possesses the ability to give shape or configuration to objects and images, has somehow turned into representing the world with too much peculiarity that is sometimes beyond the comprehensibility of people. This is perhaps the origin of experimental graphics – when a conceited designer with his idiosyncratic senses produces non-user-friendly work under the broad influence of abrupt external forces such as the cultural and technological impact.

While 'semiotic pollution' is the chaotic state of message dissemination where nuisance and offense is abstract and invisible, 'pretentiousness' is signified in the visible form of design style. Indeed design is a multi-purpose device that can be very powerful depending on the way it is used. Paul Rand says design can also be an instrument of 'disorder' and 'confusion' in addition to its well-known function of being a device for the 'expression of an idea' in a 'beautiful' form and 'useful' state (1993, 4).

Pretentious graphics sometimes are found to be fun by their 'slickly joky tone'[4] although such tone and form may not deliver the essential message. When it is over done it may have to bear responsibility in its social context. As Michael Rock puts it, 'the most socially irresponsible work is the over-designed, over-produced, typographic stunt that serves no real function.'[5]

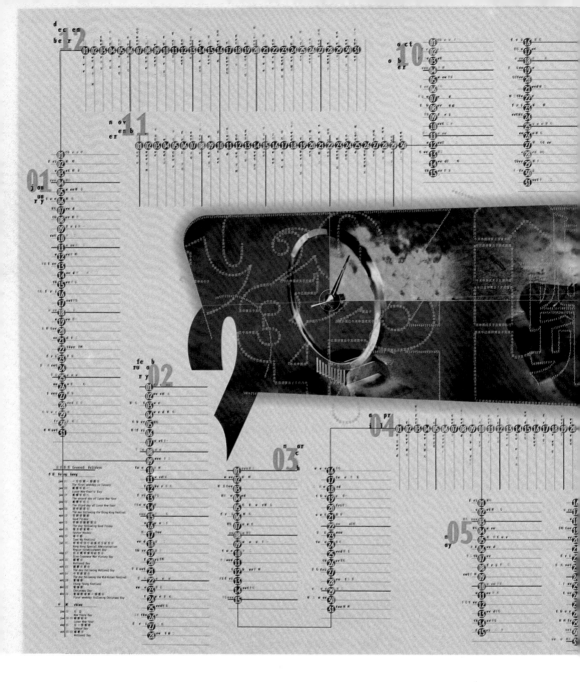

Wall calendar for Wiggins Teape (HK) Ltd. (above), a fine imported-paper supplier, experiments distorting, enlarging, reducing and layering of typographic form. Types and numbers serve as graphics and content, as well as the message (by deconstruction of the conventions of calendar layout to show a revolutionary thinking of the designer).

In terms of visual effect it is attractive and stylistic. The manipulation of dates in an unusual format is achieved at the expense of legibility. It reflects the ostentatious

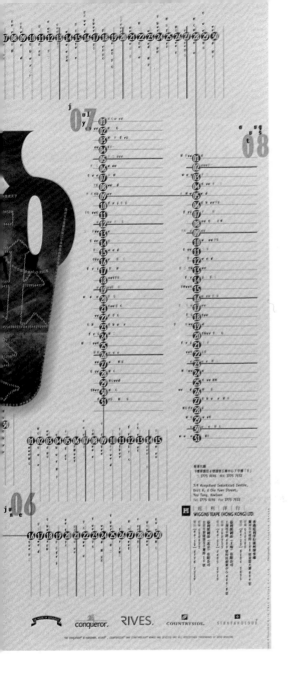

attitude of the designer who does not endeavor to inform through his work but purely aims at self-expression. He succeeds in creating a dynamic effect the calendar's practicability is questionable. The result is at odds to those people who seek to make use of the calendar. Work of this type is innovative, it acknowledges the novelty of trendy style and denounces the rule of usability – a computer-aided design in which the temptation to play computer tricks overrules the designer's ethical concern.

So understood, 'pretentiousness' is a special attitude, taste, and ethical conception of the designer that he is happy with, as Paul Rand says, 'comforted by the illusion that this must be progress . . . lack of humility and originality and obsession with style are what seem to encourage these excesses.'[6] Operationally, without best integration of graphic elements (line, space, text, picture, illustration, pattern, colour . . .) and sound principles of design (clarity, simplicity, aesthetics, understandability . . .), a 'structural failure'[7] may occur whatever the design style.

Yet 'structural success' in design is not the agenda for the day, but style-conscious novelty is. It is supposed to sweep away the boredom of conventional rigid layout giving the audience a refreshing visual excitement. But the stress on style is just part of a design that is best supplemented by solid meaning. In 1984, Dilnot called attention to the narrow focus on professional design activity, the emphasis on solitary genius-creators, and the fetishization of design as a 'value' expressed through style.[8]

Although style-emphasis demonstrates vagueness, creates uncertainty, the complex look may satisfy the vanity of the designer, if this is the objective at all. Today, as the goal of design is moving towards what is new, but not what is good, experimental style is likely to dominate graphic design, facilitated by computer technology.

Technology Intervention: Practice, Ideation, Style

The influence of computer technology on design is radical and profound. Today, across all design disciplines, the use of the digital tool is inevitable. It is the direction in which the whole industry is moving. Technology literally challenges graphic practice (the way images are manipulated), the ideation (the way we initiate and think about those images) and last but not least, the style and looks of work we produce.

In 1992, Paul Rand contended that the use of computer is believed to be 'a hindrance to invention and a barrier to the link between mind and work; the language of computer is the language of technology, it is also the language of production, but not the language of design.'

Is his assertion being overturned by the current mass visual communication almost wholly constructed on the desktop computer? To most designers, if not all, the computer has become the language of design.

Using this fast digital tool, however, we excel in 'manufacturing', but not necessarily 'designing', visual images, because shapes and types will be generated in fine material form even if the idea is not well thought-out. The refined image quality distracts the viewer from the design quality. In this case, has the computer helped the designer to develop a new design aesthetics or has it diminished his creativity?

This argument contains an ambivalence towards the value of digital technology in our professional life. On a computer we work well in terms of efficiency (that is, time saved) and accuracy (digital drawing and configuration is precise). But from time to time, we seem to indulge in over-manipulating digital images with the abundance of graphic possibilities provided by the machine. With computer, we tend to manufacture visual chaos that brings the viewer an undesirable visual experience – 'comprehension and readability difficulty', offended/irritated emotion' and/or 'sensibility confusion' as mentioned earlier in this book.

This is why computerized-graphics is often considered problematic. Although some designers argue that the computer is used purely as a tool yet it is beyond our consciousness to be any wiser in terms of exercising control over the machine for most of the time. While technological options are unlimited and their handiness irresistible, we tend to immerse ourselves in 'computerthought', to produce 'computerwork' which appears in a 'computerlook'.

Many designers rely on machine capability rather than personal sensibility in designing that a lot of their work look somewhat like demonstrations of imaging program exhibiting the power of digital tools – human dependence on technology is revealed.

One may ask: while computer manipulation now replaces conventional handicraft, are the designer's mental and manual skills now replaced by computer skill? This may be so when instant graphics or a clip art image replace a commissioned artist's handskill; in truth, it is not: the computer enables the making of visual-gadgetry but does little to inspire ideas.

A magazine page, which is designed with an experimental approach, using full range of features provided by a page-making program exemplifies computer intervention on design ideation and style.

Content page of a Hong Kong computer magazine, *Learning Mac* (right). As a computer-learning magazine the design should have an innovative look but it appears to be typographically illiterate only. Editorial content can hardly be read – a result of free transformation of form and type and color manipulated on the computer.

Such approach is popular in editorial design of music and fashion, youth and popular culture magazine worldwide. The phenomenon may be common for some youth magazines whose editorial direction is not clear, so, perhaps 'letting the designer do his own thing,' (1997) is the way, as Poynor puts it in his article on *Ray Gun*. This local design reflects the ideology of Hong Kong young designers: to express oneself by a new form of visual gesture. While they consider the clarity and purity of classical modernist style 'too corporate, inflexible and limiting,'[9] they turn to embrace the pretentious language of new wave design. They believe that 'there is no standard, there should not be any standards, anything can be possible'[10] in the contemporary design world.

Even though the compositional style demonstrated by *Learning Mac* is intended, it has become somewhat cliches. While it seeks to be outrageous in the belief that it is the right tone to address to a particular audience (the young computer users), the construction of irrational layout is nevertheless a malfunction (and a deviated ethics) of design.

This phenomenon, visualized by pictorial and textual codes serviced by technology, however is queried by Manzini, 'What are the anthropological implications of the widespread penetration of technological science on the products of our life' (1992, 219)? Manzini argues that there has to be an ethics of design adequate to deal with the new problematic framework and to address new sensibilities.

and the names contained in this
are the properties of their respective
companies. Our aim is no intention to
promote or demote or
presence in a...
ence of our readers...
reserved...
reproduction...
storage...

※編者話
※正在發想編者話有什麼好講，要到放飛鄴拿來一本新鮮出爐的MaxPxxx

好高興呀！

做乜看事呀，咁嘢話呀？其係咖，講乜咁多期慘事，搏同情都要曬杯。世事都係得咁笑，炸爆炸到反肚又點，遲早你都要散你，發晒神經又會不知苦笑一下。電台個DJ話買Mac超過夢十萬八萬蚊，PowerMac又係會咁會出：咁又點？唔通你又打電話上去嗎又吹，但唔肯話買Eurythm Annie Lennox係男抑女，不過吹吓架啫，人哋話三年後就會做哂用咖神咮。從頭睇過，咁又點？你咪都試過用緊System 6.07忽然嘅好7.1 Centris忽然又出咗Quadra，用緊呢600又要砍840・8100，也都慣啦，呈响度喊，哋如Apple會出新錢，唔通你現在就喺暗同維呀，唯有又笑呀「英使住」咁，成日要熱熱咗喊，未够好，然後走神拜佢說友仔嘅upgrade係要Compatible，出個Downgrade就更加慘好制。

音餅正喺，好系萬友難話時勢網編者未變長髮頭的之前流，須然到現在收埋第一卷。好系萬有人會睇到學Mac時有人手仔唔係，見到種封面D字唔見兩個字母就如過喊咭囉，好仲見番以前打工時個Engin(eer)，因臨纏做工，寫緊半個中文字嗰啦低誰在人，一樣咁開心！又好系萬有人嘅嘅字多過本學Mac（咁好唔嘢！喺有人手吖嘛）！——Sorry！Sorry！下次開啦大家得咗笑喋，不過各位學加學Mac嘅自字比賽，千其唔好咁嗌隔喊大哋條實系嘅*），更加系萬書中加嗰講讀題嗰，你加也帝叫做Meun，七你做Shaned Library，也帝科做Shootcut Key呢？嗰係目日玩 South C Cross Word Puzzle，都幾考吓，最何博番嗰中塞無例出題底，可喺下斌哆？

如要各位知有兩段接受以上的挑戰，梗快快去買番本MisPrint喋！

哩完人嘟，又講番自己？今期信嗰，依然係嘅滿編，不係不爭部份抽睇，嘆位讀者見弇！今期的稿同友讀免使人諗地咭裡視業D字傈大家嗰，如嗰嘅來信分嘅，越哋大嘅文章，希望大家好似老編一樣，睇到嗰嗰到滿到嗰地，就不得不提出一些各位在來信之時要注意之事嗰（中唔快D講嘟吓Notes）

1、寄到咁急萬分火燒眉嗰，請盡量不要打電話來，盡量諳用fax／一嘶要系編部時咗到仔？二嘶：個客火起版即時大喊：「有無爆X錯，做咁成咗X程，點收返呀！！」
老編（正職切藍花）低聲限風之際、電話喋：「喂、老編呀？我買Mac好好呀？」

答案：實部都達利喋。
2、Fax來之時，請清楚注明Fax No.、Tel No.及地址。
3、如果嗰話Fax同用一條線，超短注明嘅時可以fax，唔係次嘅都有接fax。
4、如果用個老來信，就唔該知會哋四圍D人，唔係阿誰接收個fax間切那，老編就要哀：「死女包」。
5、可唔可以俾三日時間老編答問題？次次嗰兩分鐘就因fax好嚇今期术得到很多讀者的自助讀緒寫文，而且個偶係係初稿，系有很多種為學Mac做工，非常多嘅，今期可能未用到第下，下種就要到下你我哋已經將你稿入晒錄名單，以後陸續睇到（——1）、嘅之具唔咗時專嘅。

各位亦可以看到今期文章內容嘅區，有Games・Spreadsheet、M ResEdit等等、新奇突破DTP的框框，如果有萬人被刀相助以後一定Multimedia・Animation・Data Base等等。

最後好嚟囉飽（少有喔！），祝大家學Mac越步，凡事開心，大家得晚係。
**好多謝Vincent兄幫手，學Mac步入PowerMac時代喔，以後可！
PowerMac睇啦！

—者話—

The Hong Kong Experience of Technology in Design

It is not easy for any design community to develop ethics of design adequate to deal with the upcoming technological and cultural impact. Especially in Hong Kong where a short-sighted and profit-oriented norm dominates the profession, the practice of design ethics is side-tracked by the impact of technology. In fact, Hong Kong in its current context is typical of the 'post-industrial' metropolis which, according to Ezio Manzini, is 'the "global village" that extended across planet, whose characteristics are conspicuously marked by the diffuse and profound impact of new technologies' (1992, 221).

Technology brings an increase in mass audience communication channels which involve a growth in the need for visual design. Graphic work now has an even bigger, more critical audience to address, to reach and to affect. However, Hong Kong is historically immature in its design culture which, in the earlier years, is conservative to new sensibilities – the Hong Kong experience of technology is therefore a unique and difficult process.

Visual presentation in most media, now seen drowning the city, has prospered just in the past 3 decades. Henry Steiner, an early foreign design professional in Hong Kong, describes the condition, standard of design and typesetting business in 1961 as 'primitive'. He recalls, 'Basically, it [the design profession] was nonexistent . . . there was even no concept of typesetting as a separate business . . . there was no notion of specialization at all. That was in the day when Chinese newspapers were set character by character by hand.'[11]

30 years later in Hong Kong technical advancement in design production and its peripheral business is tremendous: computer work stations are extensively used in design studios; color separation and printing services are among the best in Asia; digital color proofing is now available; typesetting companies, having gone through the primitive period in the early '60s and the tough time in the '80s, have consolidated to become service bureaux providing computer output service.

The design implications of computer technology were first seen in the area of typesetting and newspaper production, where word-processing was the main task computer did. The 1970s saw the set up of many typesetting companies who imported from Japan high-performance laser typesetting machines. With the rise of the personal computer and its popularization in the '80s, when everybody who knows how to use a page layout program is able to play around with type on his own computer, typesetters ceased to develop and had to find ways for survival.[12]

The desktop publishing revolution was launched in 1985 in the United State of America. The system was introduced to Hong Kong in the late '80s. The earliest work done on these machines was of poor quality – output image pixelated, color accuracy unstable – that did not adequately reflect the original intent of the designer but accidentally generated a so-called computerized aesthetics by the coarse ragged bitmap image.

In the early 1990s when Macintosh's breakthroughs made computer capacity much more powerful, computer hardware affordable, designers (and design buyers) became excited by the hi-tech function. However, before computers were used proficiently as they are today, they were once 'an alibi for bad work', says Steiner in 1993, who condemns certain clients' response to computer graphics, 'the concept can be nil, the execution vapid, but it's okay because it's computer technology' (1993, 21).

The current state of graphic technology is sophisticated: not only by utilizing computers are 2-dimensional visual objects produced for traditional carriers, like posters, books and magazine, but the screen is a new means of carrier serving the function as did its predecessor, the paper page. Interface design on interactive communication media is as hot in town as in other places across the world.

The Web has become a familiar medium. Many Hong Kong companies and organizations are keen on launching a web site on the internet; magazines and newspapers, apart from appearing in printed form, now 'go electronic' – having an online edition. 'The website represents a cost-efficient medium to advertise products and services,' says Paul Mottram of Asia Sources Media Group. He claims that 'websites focus on a very targeted audience – people go to it for a specific reason'.[13] But it is also true that we are always annoyed going through tangled hierarchies of elements, scrolling horizontally and vertically searching, or are frustrated by graphic disorder appearing on the screen. Although the clutter during navigation is understood as the way Web application works, weak graphic execution is main reason.

Achieving visual rhythm in the cyber-space is a responsibility of the web designer. In graphic design for the World Wide Web, operational and technical limitations make the balance of text and images even harder to accomplish. Yet legibility and design aesthetics are as important in this screen-based media as in printed page.

Designers working on this platform, which is so different from the artboard, pen and ruler that they used to work with, incline to playing with layered interfaces rather than to representing messages modestly and aesthetically by an considerate editorial mind. As noted in *Eye* by Max Bruinsma, who investigates interface design and graphic design for electronic media, says, 'in the domain of new media we can observe a shift from the concern for form to the concern for structure' (1993).

The quality of locally-designed homepages varies. Given that a number of consulting groups serve to help incorporate traditional techniques into web-construction for corporate sites, the classic aspects of graphic design in the structure, layout and form of websites are the task of graphic designer.

Interactive design involves psychological and sensory, even physical aspects of the user who reacts more directly and instantly than to other media. A pertinent attitude towards human receptivity as well as aesthetic considerations of visual presentation on the screen is nevertheless essential, as in conventional graphic design on the printed page.

The Hong Kong experience of technology in design has gone through a tough time at the cost of failing to focus on originality and creativity, although it is well-known for efficiency. The integration of the new technology into our creative practice is irreversible. Understanding our design culture in a historical perspective, perhaps, may help to devise a direction to adapt to the present, as well as future design environment.

NOTES

1. Robin Kinross, *Fellow Readers*, 1996.

2. See 'Graduation Fever', *Hinge*, 1995, Vol. 227, p. 44-45 for comments on Hong Kong design students' work and attitude.

3. Jan van Toorn, *"And Justice for All . . . "*, 1994, p. 147.

4. A. McRobbie, 1994, p. 15

5. Michael Rock condemns irrational typographic treatment, *Looking Closer: Critical Writings on Graphic Design*, 1996, p. 3.

6. Paul Rand, 'Confusion and Chaos: The Seduction of Contemporary Graphic Design', *Design Culture: An Anthology of Writing from the AIGA Journal of Graphic Design*, 1997, p. 120.

7. Peter Dorma suggests that a designer is basically not responsible for the 'structural failure' of a product (which is the work of the engineer) but shares responsibility in the 'human/machine interface' only. *Design since 1945*, 1993, p. 11. I see the graphic designer's role encompassing the design structure (the way type and images are laid out, the execution of an idea) and human reaction. He is the one liable for any 'structural failure'.

8. Dilnot's concept cited in 'Good History/Bad History', *Looking Closer: Critical Writings on Graphic Design*, 1994, p. 224.

9. Rick Poynor, 'Type and Deconstruction in the Digital Era', *Looking Closer: Critical Writings on Graphic Design*, 1994, p. 84.

10. Neville Brody, *Typographic Design No. 2*, 1994.

11. Richard Lawrence, 'Hong Kong on the Brink', *Print*, 1993, p. 21.

12. A Hong Kong typesetting company claims that it was in the mid-70s when Hong Kong witnessed an economic boom from which the typesetting business did benefit. Indirectly serving the commercial sectors, it received orders from printing and advertising agencies who did publicity and promotion of all kinds of activities. Investment was made to equip the company with advanced phototypesetting machinery. However, from the late '80s through the '90s, they experienced a fall of business in typesetting and have turned to providing computer output service instead.

13. Source: *Media*, May 1998, p. 12.

5

Design Culture Vs. Trading Culture

Design in the Trading Economy

Meanwhile, in the shift of cultural and technological conditions, people are confronted with contemporary graphics amid a contradiction: we find the new and dynamic look of modern graphics attractive but we tend to be irritated by the uncertainty, inhumanity and insincerity that come along with it. Such a development is greatly influenced by Western design trend, yet there are also underlying factors such as the local trading culture that has contributed to determining the mode of operation and manifestations of Hong Kong graphic design.

So these problems (in both graphic and product disciplines) can be summed up as consequences of first, historically, an immature design culture where 'taste' and 'originality' are ignored (or discouraged); secondly, prevailing trading economic strategies that devalued the profession; thirdly, contemporary cultural impact from the West that influenced design thinking; and fourthly, technology of the information age that altered real practice.

Among them, the trading economy and 'taste' of people are two inherent (and inherited) sources of problems indigenous and unique to Hong Kong. The focus of this section will lie on the historical evidence of design in the trading economy derivative of these combination factors.

Under their influence designers and manufacturers lost sights of the goal of design: they dismissed originality and innovation working purely with export-oriented objectives and low-cost/cost-competitive strategies. Gradually, everyone involved in this 'production culture', lost also the ability to see how the disadvantage of merely making mimetic objects can affect the long term development of a Hong Kong identity. Such an attitude characterizes the design culture of Hong Kong.

Design culture & immature design culture

It is impossible not to talk about the design culture of a place[1] in the attempt to explore its human and economic implications. The notion of design culture, according to Manzini, refers to the involvement 'in the act of planning and projecting, where not only the designer, but everyone is engaged in bringing an idea to fruition – denoting a more cooperative activity than one in which the designer acts as a lone individual.'[2]

If what Manzini identifies is an idealistic state of design profession which actively involves itself in working towards a better result with other people in the society, particularly those of the business sector, then Hong Kong design must be surviving in an 'immature' design culture in which, designers are somewhat isolated operators of a repressing trading policy.

To say it is 'immature' first I mean the unawareness (or unconsciousness) among designers, of their possible contribution and responsibility in the functional and representational aspects of design ever since the early 1950s when the so-called 'design' business first emerged. This indifference is the major and triggering reason for the poor quality of Hong Kong design.

It is 'immature' also for its social status: design is considered peripheral in the economy, traditionally not given the same respect as other professions, nor its potentiality to help in developing a design-led civilized advanced society (like that of Italy and Japan), been realized. Design is literally under-used, designers' creativity constrained.

Trading culture

With this social perception Hong Kong economic activity involves little of designers' innovative input. To understand why, we need to look at the trading background against which design operated. Hong Kong started to produce export designs in the late 19th century. It was not until the middle 20th century that the notion of advertising was first introduced, that graphic design took shape and started to flourish (Turner, 1990).

But it did so under conditions laid down by commercial strategies adapted to the demands of overseas markets. According to Turner, 'Hong Kong was the direct descendent of a unique system of design and manufacturing that had established itself over the centuries along the commercial thoroughfares of the Pearl River delta' (1990, 8).

That system was adopted by industries operating in coastal provinces of South China as well as those in the Hong Kong context. The characteristics of economic strategies of these regions were first a labor-intensive production, secondly, a strong export orientation – making goods to order from Western buyers and thirdly, a process of adaptive design – highly flexible in response to buyer's needs.

In design terms the second and third attitudes of the past have determined the fate of contemporary design with the ideology passed down to today's practice. Both in the past and at present Hong Kong's style of design adaptation favors a stress on short-term trading advantage, thus no long-term commitment nor expectation to any design is anticipated – the culture of 'adaptability without principles' was created.

'Adaptability-without-principle'

'Adaptability without principle' as social norm governed the making of objects in a broad sense. From an economic view, to maintain adaptability is a simple way to maintain competitiveness, a necessary approach in a colonized social and trading situation such as that of Hong Kong.

Design practices, having to adapt to varying demands of buyers, tend to ignore some principles of design – originality, harmony, beauty and aesthetics. In the presence of adaptability, the so-called designs embrace faddism, insincerity or ugliness, which results in crucial implications on the value of designed objects we made and the role of designers who made these objects.

Matthew Turner characterizes export-oriented designs of the early 20th century: 'The quality, variety, and sophistication of designs destined for overseas consumption may be taken as entirely a matter between the producer and the buyer . . . with which the rest of society has no connection.'[3]

Probably Hong Kong designers have not chosen to act as 'lone individuals' but as recorded in our short history of design,[4] they are confined to working on imposed order, they find no access to the more advanced knowledge of design, nor space for the expression of ideas in this circumstances. Their design thinking (the mind set) and design skill (the practice) tend to become retarded, design outcome embodies no essence, nor spirit of design.

What ensues is an infamous reputation – Hong Kong design is considered 'lack of imagination,'[5] while Turner mentions the Western view of Hong Kong design in the mid-nineteenth century, 'Hong Kong workers were capable of producing acceptable designs if, however, "copies are made of designs furnished from abroad"', [and], 'locally manufactured products are [just] described as "fantastic in design", "odd", "coarse", "peculiar" or "inferior".'[6]

It is clear that trading-led design strategies tend to exploit creativity into producing low-quality (cheap) novelties. Adaptation strategy, in this sense, brings short-term profit to the overall economy but exacerbates design inability.

'Adaptability-without-principle' in the graphic profession
Traditionally 'adaptability without principle' took effect mostly on product-making due to the great needs of this type of goods in foreign markets. But there is a continuity of such an attitude in both product and graphic design in the present days. While in the modern setting manufacturing industries are still largely export-led, graphic design, the supporting service, nevertheless has to adopt given styles as was done before. There is no difference for the graphic profession to practice 'adaptability without principle', both in the reproduction and representation aspects, which is, to adapt ourselves not only to types of design but styles of design.

An approach bearing some of the above attitudes becomes conspicuous in local industries – the 'hustle' strategy,[7] flexibility in responding at high speed to new and emerging trends. The strategy is popular for it allows our versatile capability and resources to be integrated for commercial purposes. Unavoidably in this modern trading culture design is forced to operate without long-term commitment to outcome nor to the profession.

In fact a lot of graphic design firms, from advertising-based to manufacturer-affiliated, currently play a role mainly as packagers – to adapt design to the varieties of styles the markets need and to meet demand in terms of delivery time. Enright quotes the words of a manager in the manufacturing sector, 'We accept unreasonable requests, and then we deliver' (1997, 49). Such 'false' commitment is absurd for it undermines the value of design and frustrates the profession.

That the notion of 'adaptability-without-principle' prospers in our trading culture is critical because arising from it is a series of linked consequences and implications that affect the whole of Hong Kong design development.

Adaptability without Principles: Consequences

The cult of imitation

The condition of imitation and adaptation in our society is painful. Despite rising affluence and easy access to a richness of material and technical resources by which designers are expected to practice innovation, the idea of imitation and adaptation is still pervasive.

I see the imitation culture more as a collective ideology of the majority population than as a real need. The way counterfeit merchandise and fake goods are made, traded and used, is not at all considered bad by most Hong Kong people who have little understanding of the value of design originality. Perhaps this is why there is always a local market to accommodate the dumping of pirate versions of entertainment compact disks, handbags, designer label luxury goods – probably a consequence of poor civic education in Hong Kong.

The ideology of imitation affects not only products, but other design forms like packages, advertising and printed material where graphic design plays a significant part in giving fake products a package.

Technically the imitation climate in graphic area is backed up by a modernized and fast-developing printing industry equipped with an abundant supply of imported paper stock, packaging material and machinery. Imitation examples are found in graphics of stationery, toys and novelties which I call 'graphic kitsch' – pretentious graphic objects appropriating established licensed brands.

Hong Kong's capacity to produce, export and re-export pirated goods has been well-known to the rest of the world for a long time. Although recently the United States of America listed Hong Kong as among the top four sources of fake goods[8]. The exploitation of foreign licensed characters in local and China-made products was even more serious back in the 1980s, before the concept of intellectual property protection was promoted and the tight control over copyright enforced by the Hong Kong government.

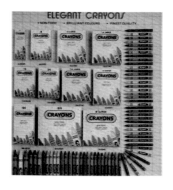

Two ads appearing in local trade magazine *Hong Kong Enterprise* during the 1980s exemplifies the phenomenon of imitation in local manufactured products for export (left). One ad shows a copy version of Swiss famous-brand 'Caran D'ache' color pencil package and the use of licensed cartoon character 'Snoopy' on another pencil case design. Another shows that the graphic identity of American brand 'Crayola' crayons, is copied by local brand 'Elegant Crayons'.

Designer's Role in the Cult of Imitation

To borrow visual properties of other culture indicated an unreserved attitude to copying by 'replication', 'duplication', an idea initiated by Hong Kong manufacturers but executed by designers. Having to work under the strict limits of export-orientation, designers were deprived of the opportunities in the cultivation and expression of individual taste – the ability to judge. The Western view of the Chinese designer – he who possessed no principles of design[9] was molded in our repressive past.

Designers were bound to adapt to imposed ideas under trading constraints. Today the repression is moderating, but the enthusiasm to copy foreign designs seems not to lessen. Although it seems natural that we envy, and strive to imitate the imported style of living, fashion and the like, imitation is nevertheless disgraceful but with regard to creativity.

Whether the act of simply 'borrowing' other people's concepts as reference, an infringement of design is controversial, yet the copying, faking, stealing of a total image definitely is a dishonor. Despite this, making adaptations to patented brand names, logos, graphics and licensed characters, or copying the established image, form and structure of the original, is a common practice in Hong Kong, like the 'Tempo' incident which has lasted for over 15 years still the subject of an on-going imitation.

'Tempo' paper handkerchief and its eighteen imitation versions (right). Matthew Turner in *Made in Hong Kong* captions this illustration, 'Copying rather than adaptation, was to characterize the transition period from the decline of an early modern style until the more recent rise in confidence among the new generation of Hong Kong designers' (1990, 79).

It was 1990 when Turner made this remark by which he implies that it is a design phenomenon in the transition period between the past and present state of Hong Kong design. Today, perhaps to his disappointment, copying still dominates over origination. Copying is considered pragmatic, so conceived, few care to develop new brands and and new identity in the belief that there is no room for them to survive in the marketplace nor overseas buyers be interested in new brands other than established ones.

The Kleenex 'Scott' paper napkin package and its imitation versions provide a good example of imitation for local market. The graphic design of 'Jumbo' box-tissue and 'Sunday' box-tissue (below) are identical to 'Scott' except for the brand name which is sometimes hard for purchasers to differentiate. 'Jumbo' is sold at 10 dollars for 3, 'Sunday' 8 dollars for 3 while 'Scott' at 12 dollars each.

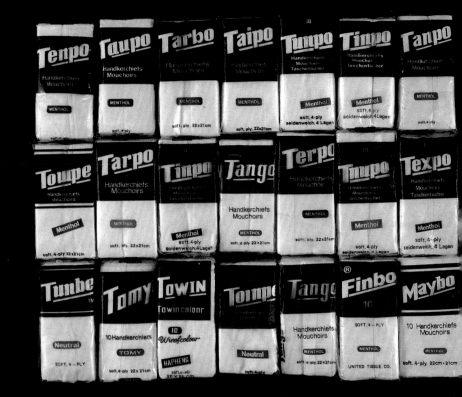

'Commercial' Design

In Hong Kong, imitation, kitsch and unprincipled adaptation bloom under the umbrella of 'commercial' design, a term that alludes to an opposite meaning of 'professional'.

The interpretation (rather than literary meaning) for 'commercial' in graphic design has always been degrading. In Western design history, 'commercial' art is widely interpreted as a practice that 'catered to the lowest common denominator of taste'.[10] Recently the term 'commercial' with regard to design is understood as follow: 'Knowledge of modern aesthetics and theories of functional communication distinguished the new discipline of design from traditional 'commercial' art which was provided to businesses directly by printers'.[11]

As a stream of 'commercial' design methods, adaptation, which ignores the principles of design by adopting trading principles originated from the need of early Hong Kong export goods and soon established itself as a particular ideology and mode of operation. In 1997, Enright identifies one of the advantages of Hong Kong export traders as the ability to elaborate and develop existing models of merchandise, but 'their strengths are in interpretive, rather than original, design.'[12]

Enright's remarks exposes the limitations of design input in the industry. In fact commercial principles, if considered carefully, could work as mediators for the expansion of design power to benefit the society and economy as a whole. However, the orientation of Hong Kong entrepreneurs have determined the unique specialities of Hong Kong design – as the 'interpreter'. The 'interpretive' policy that once benefited Hong Kong economic performance (and still does if one inclines to the complacency of the current position as the 'packager'[13] only), did not reflect a satisfactory improvement in the development of a healthy design profession.

Retarded development of design profession

What is initially called the design profession first took shape in small-scale 'commercial' design settings by synthesizing foreign influences and local human and material resources. They claimed to provide a wide range of services, from a label design to packaging and modification of export ornamental objects, toys, even interior decoration and contracting work.

Development of the profession was retarded when such a diversity of commitments converged under a single establishment that is fairly limited in its capacity – the lack of design knowledge and design equipment.

Being market-driven, design has no specialization, no professional constraint, no motivation nor aesthetic aspiration. The opportunity for great graphic works to appear, or to survive, is diminished under such conception and condition if it exists at all.

The quality of graphic kitsch is distressingly poor due to the above factors. Gradually overseas buyers are convinced that 'authentic', 'true' and 'original' forms and ideas are missing in Hong Kong design; they are accustomed and receptive to such quality and standard as long as the goods are traded at a low price.

Aldersey-Williams in *World Design*, accuses winning designs of Hong Kong watches and clocks, some of them works of students, for lacking originality. He puts it, '[these watch designs] bear more than a passing resemblance to existing but more expensive watches and clocks from abroad. . . In keeping with recent tradition, their designs are strangely familiar. Why is this? Do the students not feel ashamed?' (1992, 132) – a severe indictment of our future designers' design ethics.

George Sowden, a judge for Hong Kong Designers Association's Design Show 1996, criticizes the entries, 'I adopted a firm, on the whole, critical attitude to all those entries which in some measure, albeit with great precision of form and attention to details, failed to suggest any direction which design can evolve . . . What a large number of entries lacked was 'thoughts, lifestyles and innovative cultural preference'.[14]

That design profession is retarded even in the contemporary context is undeniably true. In fact resistance to recognizing the value of the profession and design originality can be traced back some four decades, when the fluctuating social and economic conditions in the difficult years of the 1950s and '60s became unfavorable to the idea.

Hong Kong was more affluent in the 1970s soon after recovering from the political and social crisis in 1967.[15] Opportunities arose for design practice to attempt innovation with the aid of upcoming technology and government support,[16] yet the majority of business leaders inclined to the tradition of copying and imitation, by which their trading profit presumably could be secured.

In this manner, the culture of adaptation and imitation was retained. Although at a later stage, instead of pure imitation which allowed no more innovation, design production shifted to the strategy of 'modification'. It was a relatively constructive model by the 'research and development' process which was adopted in a number of leading manufacturing companies since the 1980s.

Such reform seems to offer more room for creativity in the restructured working system, but the social condition and public cognition of the necessity of design reform is inadequate leading to a lack of professionalism.

Lack of professionalism
Design professionalism can be established only when recognition is sought from the greater community, that is to say, in a mature design culture in which the practice, having performed professionally, could express itself and be accommodated. But our past experience in the pursuit of professionalism makes that sound unlikely.

According to Steiner, Hong Kong graphic design in 1961, 'was an unformed profession, it was 'commercial' design that was working'. He describes the rough, low-quality 'commercial' design as a result of the 'dim sum' approach by which the designer would present plenty of design options for the selection of the customer but, most of them contain 'nil' concept and 'vapid' execution'.[17]

In the last decade Hong Kong graphic design started to find a place on the international stage of design: a handful of brilliant designers managed to establish a good reputation for Hong Kong. As Lawrence states, 'they are able to produce higher quality work which is up to the international standard'[17] But does this imply a satisfactory condition of the design profession as a whole – when the successful designers represent just a small proportion of total design establishments in the territory?

We must admit, in general, a great number of design practitioners are not quite professional, due to historical reasons and educational background – design was badly developed and design education literally non-existent until the recent few decades.

Though design grew rapidly from the 1960s to '80s, when Hong Kong saw the flourishing of manufacturing industry, the discipline had no inspiration of its own and retreated to be purely supportive of other industries. Consequently a problem emerged: according to Coopers & Lybrand's 1996 report on the Hong Kong design service, the industry in general suffers from an insufficient number of professionals who can advise clients in a professional manner.

The lacking of professionalism is not only derivative of economic and social conditions but of design methods and attitude. One's design attitude reflects one's inclination about the appropriate choice, and configurations of design. It is an exercise of taste. So the problem of taste, the failure of judgement and reflection in the course of designing is a significant factor as well as a consequence of the various unfavorable design phenomenon discussed in the preceding section.

The Problem of Judgement in Design

Taste and Design

As suggested earlier, design problems arising from adaptability-without-principle are consequences of an export-orientated trading economy, an immature design culture and the designer's disoriented attitude. Hence they are technical and cultural as well as human issues. The latter indicates the lack of taste among people involved in design activities.

Moreover, if the Western view of Hong Kong design standard is sustainable; that it is inferior inferior and imitative; lacks imagination and is low-quality, then it perhaps alludes to our lack of taste too.

DESIGN CULTURE VS TRADING CULTURE

As discussed, in Hong Kong visual culture, there is a cult of imitation in which designer's taste is embodied. Not only in design for manufactured goods, but in a variety publications, advertising materials and environmental graphics, one sees the celebration of deliberate imitation.

For example, a popular icon in American culture, the poster on the recruitment of army, 'I Want You' created by James Montgomery Flagg in 1916 was recently copied for local use. In public areas, on buildings and structures there always displayed peculiar taste of designers in their use of hybrid visual elements. Some pedestrians on the Wan Chai street perhaps will have noticed the huge wall of a restaurant building decorated by an allegedly artistic tile mosaic with an visual effect resembling the 'nonobjective' painting. 'Composition with Red, Blue, and Yellow' by French artist, Piet Mondrian in 1930. More interesting is that the mural is located under a Chinese-style roof structure adjacent to the Great Wall motif. Whether they clash with each other or give a special cross-cultural flavor to the environment is debatable.

Without the ability of judgement and discrimination, a designer may produce unintelligible or dreadful design. To improve, it requires a broadening of mind, like the cultivation of taste in the designer, to clearly and strategically incorporate his idea in the designed objects that will illuminate.

Designed objects are indeed 'symbols and markers of ourselves and our identities', thus they are vehicles with which we show to others our judgement of things and our concern for other's judgement about our capacity of judgement and value in the world of production. Unfortunately, Hong Kong designers seem to disregard the problem of taste although it has significant relationship to design.

Design reflects a particular culture within which taste matters because it functions to externalize and materialize the inhabitants' thought style. Design is also a human/social activity which discloses the collective taste of people by the things they make and use in that particular context.

Whereas 'taste', primarily known as the ability for aesthetic judgement, plays an important part in the style and method of design used in all disciplines. The notion of taste is key in the context of designing for production, communication as well as for service. Sometimes, it is an indispensible attribute overriding technology or whatsoever.

Inasmuch as taste is inseparable from design, the relevance of taste (or the result of judgement) is important in constituting the level of design in any country, within any culture. The designer's taste determines not only the look but also the meaning of designed products/images. In Bayley's inspiring analysis, he notes, 'Taste is not so much about what things look like, as about the ideas that gave rise to them . . . we must judge the spirit that informs an object or a gesture, rather than the form of the object or the gesture itself.'[19]

Upon deeper understanding, taste represents a higher level of enriching human sensibility by the aesthetic mastering of forms and style. However, taste today is more often understood as an indicator of a person's social status and wealth (judging by the monetary value of what he uses, what he wears . . .) whereas in design it is thought to be the unusual, radical ways of thinking and practical treatment.

Truly taste is embodied in one's preference (or inclination) for material life (the place to live, the food to eat, the fashion to wear) in the commodity world by which it seems to suggest that the pursuit (or possession) of the expensive/newest versions of things and objects proves one has good taste of a certain kind.

Such social perceptions of taste is universal and a tradition but there is a definition problem with respect to design if one confines oneself to this understanding. In design context, taste (or the judgment and discrimination ability) should not be always directed to trendy and visible things.

Apparently, what is demonstrated in the act of consumption as taste (of a group or an individual) tends to change as one's value of the commodity shifts. My conviction is: what we should look for in design as taste, is something ethical, spiritual, symbolic, a timeless attribute to the welfare of human beings' mental state and physical reaction, like a designed image that articulates a complicated message through a strategic visual presentation, or a well-thought product design that benefits user experience.

This is to say, taste as an abstract quality has yet to be concretized –
by projection or representation by design in order to function. However, the
process – to apply one's taste onto design – is adventurous under the impact
of different forces of the modern world – technological, cultural, even
political. How to grasp good taste and act in good taste requires a journey of
cultivation, without it, the lack of taste simply produces distressing work as
one can see in Hong Kong design.

The lack-of-taste

Looking retrospectively into the design history of Hong Kong, the 'lack-of-
taste' is evident. During the early 20th century when the western countries
saw the explosion of 'modern'[20] design, in Hong Kong, the so-called 'design'
operation was still in its infancy and adaptation was the mode of practice.
Design and manufacture of goods were adapted to meet the needs of
overseas markets by following specifications given.

According to Turner, graphic elements appeared on export works of
those days ranged from traditional Chinese drawings to foreign motifs. He
puts it: 'Victorian' imagery; Chinese Lingnan paintings, and European styles
from Art Nouveau and Art Deco were used; as were motifs borrowed from late
Meiji and Taisho Japan' (1990, 9).

Adaptive styles may easily turn any goods into 'kitsch'[21] like the
above-mentioned in which 'lack-of-taste' become evident to viewers. 'Lack-of-
taste' comprises innocence of aesthetic conception and the thoughtlessness
in bring people pleasure by humanistic design. Practically it refers to the
insensible appropriation of borrowed images, theoretically the separation of
form and function, that which regards truth as irrelevant, that which
mindlessly imitates, that which fragments the message, that which projects
an obscurity of design identity.

Failure of judgement and reflection (of the appropriateness of design
decision) in graphic design may lead to visual ineffectiveness
(misinformation, being offensive or irritating to the eyes and mind of the
reader). One sees a loss of aesthetics, originality and sincerity in works like
these, yet somehow they are common qualities of Hong Kong generic
graphics.

Hong Kong design culture has yet to be reconstructed to confront the deeply-rooted manufacturing concept that represses creativity. But the lack-of-taste (and the unconsciousness of it) among people is also distressing: it is as critical as the imposed trading ideology.

Taste and design in Hong Kong
Given the immense political, economic and cultural changes over the last century, Hong Kong design, which exposes national taste, seems not to have changed much. Historically in Hong Kong the relevance of taste is either ignored or underestimated leading to sub-standard export design. In the contemporary days, the exercise of taste, the reflection of judgement in the design spheres invites criticism.

It seems that the introduction of remarkable design technology to the practice, the recent popularization of design education have not been able to cultivate the taste of people. Although taste may be inherited, it can also be acquired. But if our design culture does not have a goal as what Manzini calls, 'habitable', to become 'a cooperative activity among designers and everyone engaged . . .', it will continuously lead to more design failure.

A household utensils ad (preceding page) placed in *Hong Kong Enterprise* of the mid-1990s. Targeted at local trading agencies as well as foreign buyers, it features a heap of low-market export products in a chaotic visual presentation. An archetype of visible bad taste. Perhaps a marketing strategy to represent the merchandise as cheap items to appeal to potential customers. Despite, from a design perspective, a better treatment could be applied for the same purpose, now it reveals only the bad taste of the designer and certainly, of the advertiser and buyers.

Surely good taste or bad taste is never an easy thing to define. In fact it is impossible to define except in a particular context with a defined standard. Taste and design alike are both subjective but from a human perspective the extent to which psychological pleasure is achieved through 'appropriate' judgement and execution of design is a reflection (as well as function) of a designer's good taste.

Hong Kong graphic design that manages to reflect good taste is a rarity, whereas idiosyncratic, personal expression by design is always rationalized as having 'taste'. The production of kitsch graphics and imitative visual objects that imply bad taste, is depressingly common. This is passed on as a part of our historical design experience and proliferates today. The tendency that the imitation and adaptation ideology of the trading culture is unlikely to be replaced by new ideas challenges the role of contemporary designers.

Rethinking Designer's Role in the Trading Culture

Rethinking adaptation

In speaking of adaptation, one immediately associates it with some negative implications. Yet the idea is not necessarily incompatible with design, it is just the Hong Kong style of mindless adaptation that is problematic. In some cases there is a necessity and advantage for such an approach that tends to lead to good results. Professor John Heskett, in his seminar at Hong Kong Polytechnic University in October 1996, said that craft people do not always try to invent something new, they derived their design from experience. When it works well, it does not need to be changed.

In this sense one should adapt the design to the originality, rather than making unnecessary innovations. Thus striving for originality is nevertheless integral and important, yet when an appropriate adaptive method makes even better results, the act of adaptation and imitation is justified.

In the field of visual design, thoughtful imitation is sometimes a sound measure. Jan van Toorn defines any form of design communication as 'the imitation of earlier motifs and images . . . a product of social condition: a cultural reproduction and representation subject to the forces present in that context, which produce legitimating values and norms' (1994, 145). In order to withstand particular economic and social demands, adaptation is perhaps a significant mode of production in that context.

Rethinking packager

In being highly adaptable, Hong Kong is evaluated by Enright, optimistically, as a packager and integrator. He disagrees with the metaphor of Hong Kong as the bridge or gateway, 'Hong Kong firms are not intermediaries; they are instigators and initiators of economic activities' (1997, 54). To emphasize his belief he writes, 'Hong Kong has a particularly deep pool of talent and expertise in interpretive design . . . most often by extending and developing pre-existing fashion ideas . . . the design input of Hong Kong firms is often an important added value for customers' (1997, 55).

However, if the stated potential and capacity is substantial, Hong Kong should not be content with the role of 'packager' – one who provides services of design and prototyping at given specifications on a particular budget – but should strive for design excellence with these advantages. Although design, by nature, serves to add value and sophistication to manufactured products, the way the profession inclines to be only a subordinate seems not to be design-responsible. It is also taking the risk of becoming backward in the next decade or so: when our competing neighbors tend to challenge our economic status in the region. What then, should be our orientation for design?

Rethinking design attitude: economic reality and opportunities

Given my condemnation of the design profession it is not at all the discipline's responsibility in becoming the imitator nor its preference to give up innovation. Hong Kong design has always been dominated by the idea of imitation, an inherited, still existing social norm that becomes an obstacle to the attempt for more original and imaginative work.

To run a design business regardless of the embedded cultural and ideological tradition is both technically and geographically difficult. At this very moment, Hong Kong is still essentially an export-orientated economy despite the fairly good consumption power in the territory. But our considerable population is so small compared with the enormous overseas markets that we have to export products as well as services to other parts of the world.

Owing to this objective reason the original-equipment-manufacturing (OEM) and original-design-manufacturing (ODM) models continue, having to rely on foreign orders. The attempt to develop original-branding-manufacturing (OBM) encounters economic reality, let alone creativity problems. Economic reasons as such, in addition to problems arising from the current financial crisis, are an apparent obstacle to a radical change of attitude in design.

In 1997, the Chief Executive of Hong Kong initiated a vision for Hong Kong to become an innovation-led, technology-intensive economy in the 21st century for the region. To realize the vision there will be investment and facilitation on relevant industries.[22]

Specifically, it is envisaged to turn Hong Kong into 'a world-class design and fashion centre.'[23] This is an opportunity when design (of product, graphic, fashion and service alike), as a support for a great deal of industries like entertainment and tourism, should take on a long-term strategy to develop and produce not only value-adding but value-creating (the creation of greater buyer value) works to tie in with Hong Kong's overall aspiration.

This structural shift perhaps can bring an end to the tradition of production at the lowest possible cost and a beginning for invention at the highest possible value and quality. In order to achieve the ambition, it is the determination and attitude of designers, which is most significant and that can possibly overturn the tragic tradition to discover a new Hong Kong design formula. This would be a model that is technology-based yet human-orientated, with the flavor of origination and identity. Still the resources and advantages of Hong Kong people such as flexibility and efficiency observed in trading relations can be drawn on to accelerate accomplishment of the goal.

NOTES

1. The concept of place in design history, as identified by Dennis Doordan, should not be confused with the sense of place encountered in architectural discourse. It embraces the social settings as well as the physical locale in which design occurs. Doordan, Ed., *Design History: An Anthology*, 1990. Place, in the context of this study of design culture and trading condition encompasses the region of Hong Kong and part of China where export design strategy and its ideology was first characterized since the early 20th century.

2. Ezio Manzini, 'Prometheus of the Everyday', *Discovering Design*, 1992.

3. Matthew Turner, Made in Hong Kong: *A History of Export Design*, 1990, p. 123.

4. A prevailing concept suggests there is no history of design outside the triad of Western Europe, North America and Japan, yet Matthew Turner argues, it is only by Western definition that there can be no real history of design outside the First World. Japan is quoted to show that seemingly for a country to be considered possessing a history of design, she has to be economically powerful. Hong Kong, though not regarded as being so successful as Japan, had indeed started a history of graphic design as early as 1845 when China trade artists settled and practiced in Hong Kong. Matthew Turner, 'Early Modern Design in Hong Kong', *Design History: An Anthology*, 1990, pp. 20-205.

5. Hugh-Aldersey-Williams, section on Hong Kong in *World Design: Nationalism and Globalism in Design*, 1992, p. 132.

6. Matthew Turner, 'Early Modern Design Hong Kong' *Design History: An Anthology*, 1995, p. 210.

7. A trading strategy to beat competitors to the punch by recognizing new trends more quickly and capturing a high margin of profit by being first to respond. Michael J. Enright, *Hong Kong Advantage*, 1997, p. 54.

8. 1. *Hong Kong Standard,* January 15, 1997.

9. Matthew Turner, 'Early Modern Design Hong Kong', *Design History: An Anthology*, 1995, p. 20

10. Paul Rand, *Design Forms, and Chaos*, 1993

11. Ellen Lupton, *Mixing Messages*, 1997, p. 12.

12. Michael J.Enright, Edith E.Scott, David Dodwell, *Hong Kong Advantage*, 1997, p.141.

13. Ibid., p. 80.

14. Deborah Herd, 'In Search of Identity', *South China Morning Post*, 1996.

15. China's Great Proletarian Cultural Revolution spilled over the border into Hong Kong in 1967, starting with a confrontation in March between trade unionists and a shipping company. Riots spreading across Kowloon from San Po Kong in May; demonstrators blocked roads and pro-communist activists battled police in Garden Road. In all, 52 people died during the disturbances. (Source: Hong Kong Government Annual Reports)

16. For a record of the evolution and opportunities of manufacturing industry in 1970s-80s see *The Great Achievements of Hong Kong*. 1988, pp. 55-61

17. Richard Lawrence, 'Hong Kong on the Brink', *Print*, March/April, 1995, p.21

18. Ibid.

19. Steven Bayley, *Taste: The Secret Meanings of Things*, 1991.

20. Penny Spark, *An Introduction to Design and Culture in the Twentieth Century,* 1989.

21. 'Kitsch' is a world of aesthetic make-believe and self-deception. Calinescu cited in Tester, p. 139. Hong Kong is famous for the production and export of 'kitsch'.

22. The establishment of an Innovation and Technology Fund was recommended to underline the Government's commitment and provide a secure source of funding for implementing the strategy framework. *Chief Executive's Commission on Innovation and Technology First Report*, 1998.

23. Ibid.

6

Rethinking Visual Strategies

Some Thoughts on the Function of Communication

There is an obvious observation previously mentioned in the book: contemporary graphics is questionable not only because of its eccentric look but also the deviated function of communication given by its look. Theoretically all types of visual design, including those that generate inhumanity and insincerity, do have a function but not an ethical function that brings people a pleasant sensation in their physical and semiotic environment.

Although some graphic design manufacture ideological happiness, like the images in the reality ad (p. 70), they function just to delude the reader into believing that the advertised property is full of nice features. They do not necessarily, in the end, provide what they promise aesthetically. Very often when communication functions, the audience may not get informed (of what they need to know); even if they do inform, they always inform in a way to manipulate our needs and interests, to turn us into the disoriented consumers.

'Function' has always been understood as a definition of design,[1] and 'communication', a 'function' of graphic design established between the visual object and the receiver. Visual creativity is primarily meant for enabling communication to function to a desired effect. But today it seems hard to find definite purpose in shapes and forms of contemporary visual objects: a sign with a hidden code is claimed to allow free interpretation by the individual reader but is this the goal, or an elusion of the creator who simply cannot manage to read the receiver's real needs?

Although communication is not some quantifiable substance, in design it is basically understood as transmission of some definite subject matters to somebody – a presupposed function. In this sense, are the contemporary graphics disseminating indefinite messages functioning or not? Yes, but to an unpredictable result.

Whether a design result (that is, its function) is predictable or not, it is expected to be lasting from a conventional perspective. But the most difficult thing that graphics can achieve is to provide lasting satisfaction for the audience. Yet it is only from a human perspective that 'lasting' 'satisfaction' is perhaps demanded. From a commercial view the best graphics should be ever-renewing in order to stimulate new consumption.

All visual objects do communicate something in some ways, even though what is put across does not necessarily function as intended. Unintended function is not always a failure, but this uncertainty is just the case we have to deal with in designing.

It is not my intention to say that all visual communication should be accomplished in a standardized and most efficient way (that can be boring) or deliver a single meaning at a time. As Jan van Toorn puts it, 'the concept of communication cannot be reduced to the idea of transmission of a unified meaning. The representation of reality should not be seen in such simple and linear terms' (1992, 145).

Even so, I am convinced that the urge for the means of reproduction and representation to serve a specific purpose and to function intentionally, within a particular context, is imperative especially in a disorienting world as such.

Take, for example, in the Mass Transit Railway (MTR) signage system one expects to find clarity and simplicity (practical function), whereas a MTR TV commercial certainly has emotional implications usually embodied in stylistic visual representation to tactically and effectively promote service (representational function). Both design forms function when they communicate (under designated criteria) something in their own context – the former to indicate direction, the latter arouses consumption desire. It is idealistic but not practical nor strategic that design solutions may justify their ethical existence by embodying human aspects – a 'primitive' function of 'functional' communication.

Today, apparently, the need for a 'humanistically functional' visual communication is declining. But this decline is not favorable to people in the long run. We need to arouse awareness towards diminishing people's unease in their encounters with visual objects. These measures are to take place at three levels: in the material biosphere such as the look and production of printed products, and immaterial semiosphere, as in the meaning of visual statements also in the technosphere in which man has to be able to take control of technology.

Recommendations made in the following sections are some basics of design. Therefore they can be perceived as a revival of the past, a reconciliation of the present and future design idealism, by integrating technology and human needs, in the coexistence of Western and local cultural influence.

Seemingly contradict to the current scene, I am not proposing a whole new concept at all, but suggesting a principled adaptation to current condition. Preferably with conscious ethical concern to fuse together functional and symbolic meaning of visual object. One may say that these are simply old attitudes, true – but while old attitudes are born of human needs, what the planet needs, and the society needs, they can be sustainable mode of operation in a place of ever-changing context.

For Peace of Mind: Semiotic Ecology

Earlier we spoke of semiotic pollution, the competition among ambiguous and intricate advertising message in the semiotic environment. It takes place in the course of communication, carried by physical artifacts like the printed page or electronic media like the TV screen. The term 'pollution' implies the negative implications of graphic design and advertising on people's mental dimension. Semiotic pollution involves two levels of human experience – of visible things (visual encounters of text, images and the like) and of psychological feeling (that arises in the receiving of message through visible things).

To apply the ecological metaphor to the state of graphic design I intend to emphasize the importance of making the visual environment 'habitable' for people (that resembles the green concept in the physical environment). I see the task of invoking semiotic ecology as a responsibility of contemporary designers. After all, we take part in causing the flood of messages by producing visual objects that are constitutive of cultural and social problems, we ought to retrieve a visual harmony within our capacity.

Michael Rock emphasizes the social aspect, 'The designer's social responsibility is a responsibility for creating meaningful forms. He should be conscious of the cultural effect of all products that pass through the studio' (1996, 192). Equally problematic is the exploitation of physical materials in our living environment, yet the necessity to seek an ecology in the physical context is widely understood by the society, though not well-implemented. The concern for semiotic ecology/ecology of the mind sounds conceptual thus is difficult to put into practice.

Extravagant printing specifications – for example, printing six colors with PVC lamination on both sides of a book cover finished with UV varnishing on pictures, blind embossed effect and gold stamping of company logo as well the use of bleached brilliant white paper – has serious cost (and environmental) implications. We are convinced that this is an act against environmental concern because it entails quantifiable gross exploitation of natural resources.

But how about the creators of semiotic pollution? Should they be charged for disseminating falsified message? There is silence on this issue as far as social criticism is concerned. Apparently the concept of semiotic ecology is far more difficult to articulate, than it to achieve. In chapter 3 we spoke of the indifference to human impact of graphic design which is believed to be caused by the invisibility of visual inhumanity and insincerity. And it is natural that semiotic ecology tends to be neglected, also for its invisibility.

The obstacles to establish and maintain semiotic ecology is found in current advertising strategies because moral concepts and commercial motivation conflict – mass communication materials conveys information simultaneously induce pollution in our semiosphere. In view of this Manzini argues that we need an ethics of design to deal with the diffuse production of material and immaterial artifacts from which we build the daily environment (1992, 219). This need for ethical concern, therefore, presents itself as a basis for building a 'mentally-habitable' visual world, whose condition implies semiotic ecology which is significant for our mental well-being.

Given that the ecological reading of our mind is difficult and the ecological reading of the physical environment is much easier, shall we ignore the issue of semiotic ecology but to deal with the mass of information as usual? Frankly speaking there is no definite direction or solution. After all, it is the reality that the production of semiotic refuse will continue. But in our practice, to incline to the construction of a 'mentally-habitable' world is the least a designer can contribute to improve the situation.

The term 'habitable', as defined by Manzini, refers to the environment where our existential condition should not be reduced to its functional component, but a world where human beings not merely survive but also express and expand their cultural and spiritual possibilities' (1992, 220). Where human limitations and receptivity are best observed, human desires can be expressed and people survive visual objects and advertising messages with a peace of mind, is a 'mentally-habitable' world in which an ecology of mind can be achieved.

Technology: from Visible to Invisible

It is depressingly true that technology has accelerated the pollution of our living environment. Whether digital technology has improved or denigrated the quality and value of graphic design is still controversial. The perception of this depends much on the designer's attitude towards the intervention of technology in his practice – is the computer an evil, a savior, a tool, or a partner?

Computer graphics has been criticized as idiosyncratic, self-expressive, superficial – aesthetically and culturally problematic in a sense. But to designers who have the intelligence and taste to confidently make aesthetic judgements, the computer is a convenient medium with which to produce work of as good quality as that designed with the traditional tools.

The human mind sometimes gives way to computer language. Look at the reliance young designers have on computers today: looking up clip-art imagery from a CD-rom, experimenting different configurations using available materials, whereas formal research, brain-storming, sketching out ideas and rational thinking of a philosophy behind the idea, is rarely carried out by many, if not most of them.

But if this phenomenon goes on they will find it impossible to live without the computer. Since there is every indication that the computerized mode of operation will continue, should we not reconsider our relationship with technology, in order to survive the trend?

We come across the key question: to eliminate the trace of technology or to emphasize technological beauty? To adopt the first option the reader's attention will focus on the content whilst graphic layout becomes subordinate; to exaggerate the technological look, content will be overshadowed by the surface effect. This is not at all bad because techno-graphics is not always ugly but beautiful in some instances. Anyway this second approach is prevalent in contemporary practice.

My experience (and observation) tells me that it is the designers' intent to make their works look hi-tech. The use of computer tricks and the achievement of a computer look prove their possession of computer sense and computer knowledge, to their peers, their clients, their audience. Undeniably the ability to manipulate a computer is an indispensible skill of the contemporary designer, but he is possibly driven by his intuition (which is a weakness) to become a computer person. With this thought in mind he is likely to become a slave of technology. As John Bielenberg writes in *Communication Arts*, 'Graphic designers are sometimes victims of preset patterns of thinking that inhibit them from free creativity and from truly understanding the essential nature of what they do' (1995).

The computer is neutral, though. It is not at all evil if the designer would generate forms and images with a bid for technology, simultaneously to interpret the meaning of a message with 'communication mindfulness'. Given the fact that the audience do not yield to the modest transmission of message the designer may have to incorporate the flexibility and decorative effects offered by technology.

To a certain extent, flexibility is valid in design, even in art. In Harries's discussion on the works of art, he claims, 'we must allow for complexity, tension, and incongruity, but order should triumph in the end'.[2] In my view the realm of graphic design should also accommodate vivid configurations of forms in the graphic aspect and inspiring statements in the meaning aspect. There can be contrast or rhythm, reason or paradox, whichever can best represent the idea of the designer in the interest of the reader, but not at the expense of disorder that may exploit the reader's senses. What we need is a user-friendly visual world.

As regards meaningless decorative images achieved by computer technology, I see something in common with graphic design and architectural design: even though technological beauty is refreshing, it can be short-lived if there is not a solid meaning to go with it, as we see in the postmodernist graphics. Harries remarks on some dislocated decorated fragments that now appear in so much postmodern architecture. He considers them, when first seen, interesting, when used repeatedly, what once was interesting soon becomes boring.[3]

In view of this danger, I incline to the idea of making graphic design technology-invisible. For the computer-visible work tends to reveal itself in a fragmented, ornamental look with indeterminate meaning so that its impact on the audience will not be lasting.

In 1993 Lubuz identified the dividing line among computer graphics between 'invisibility' and 'visibility'. The deliberate visible style declares the independence from the traditional approach. Practitioners resolve to produce work that explicitly looks like it was produced by a computer – coarse bitmaps and pixels as a new visual order, typographic and compositional distortion as a characteristic of postmodernist graphic design. For them, the computer is the best vehicle to generate fragmented ideas but it is also where the bad taste of the designer is revealed – images are made up of random elements without thought or skill or aesthetic implications.

In the invisible approach, the computer is used as the 'hidden machine' by which work appears fundamentally similar to 'traditional' design, taking invisible advantage of technology. My opinion is that technology should not be just invisible technically but ideologically to diminish the influence of technology design-wise – to take 'strategy' or 'concept' as the basis of design.

But there seems to be no room for these rules to function in 'visible' methods – they are always overlooked by both clients and the designer himself. Noted in chapter 4, where Steiner quotes a client's words, 'the concept can be nil, the execution vapid, but it's okay because it's computer technology'.

Since the beginning of technology intervention in the field, graphic practice has been challenged by the computer 'memory' (the capacity of a computer memory determines how sophisticated the design could be), 'program' (features of a particular software interfere with the expression of concept); 'technique' (the skill of the manipulator is sometimes taken as the skill of design); and its 'output resolution' (output quality affects the printing quality of computer-generated works).

In my view, technology will change (perhaps progress in its power may yet regress in its relationship to people) but the objectives of design will not. In order to overcome any changes in technology one should not totally rely on it. It would be sensible to use the computer purely as 'a set of sharpened tools', a 'medium of expression', a 'promising stylist' and a 'production critic', to maintain an 'invisibility' of technology in graphic design.

Rethinking Postmodern Graphics – in the Context of Hong Kong and China

One style, two contexts

Postmodernism is the culture of our time, a culture that reveals much contradiction in itself: while criticizing modernism for being too rational, too neutral, postmodernist chaotic design style very often appears as a challenge rather than as a benefit to the user. Still, the contemporary graphic designers are taking the postmodern visual strategies (layering, decentering, blurring of image, text and their meaning) so intensely. Have we not neglected the ethical function of graphic design – informing and illuminating, even gratifying? This is to react to the continual discovery in this book, of visual problems of Hong Kong posed under the strong influence of postmodernism in graphic design

It is necessary also to rethink the state of design in China given the fact that we are inherently linked in our geographical, historical, cultural context and inextricably connected in economic terms as well. The upcoming style and attitude of graphic design in both regions is under particular investigation here because Hong Kong's graphic future is definitely merging with that of China since our reunification since 1997. There is a practical (and technical) need to establishing a compatible mode of operation and communicational language.

In Hong Kong, already in 1988 Matthew Turner had written that postmodernism had opened our eyes to the importance of other forms of design, that is to say it has inspired and influenced local practitioners for more than a decade. Whereas in our motherland, since the mid-1990s in all corners of China Chinese versions of postmodern style graphics, product, architecture and interiors can be seen – the strong current of postmodernism is taking enormous effect. Regarding the phenomenon, Wang says, 'China cannot afford to miss out on design as an aspect of international competition, and it is necessary to catch up with everything new' (1999, 213).

But the Chinese (and Hong Kong) effort of catching up for something 'new' (referring to postmodern movement) is full of misunderstanding. This particular style may not be the kind of 'new' that a developing economy is hoping for, and should aim for: the basic components of postmodernism have nothing to do with innovation but are literally 'pastiche', 'retro' in terms of style, in the methods and elements used. It is usually the mix of style and historical icons (mostly from Western culture) presented in visually experimental form.

Thus Dilnot regards the current state of design in China as problematic, 'a nostalgic for a European design world is a model that looks backward; the design profession created on the basis of historic, mythic is doomed to fail' (1997). Some of his suggestions for meeting the urgent need of China such as 'origination' and to 'draw on one's own resources' (1997) are valid in all areas of design. Graphic design, in which foreign imitation has always dominating, is where our own cultural heritage should be drawn on to develop an original visual language.

The limitations of postmodernism
In this sense, perhaps we should reconsider if postmodernism is a promising strategy for design given its characteristics of pretentiousness, exaggeration and fragmentation.

Although postmodernist literary work was once claimed to be aesthetic and humanistic by the authors,[4] its perspective of things is also 'ambiguity, risk, danger, and error'.[5] These notions are problematic yet adopted in a lot of contemporary design, which therefore appears to be hostile to people. Again, it is 'a new strategy of visual representation' as a 'liberation from the dead weight of exhausted modernism,'[6] it is not meant for caring for people in the first place. Not surprisingly the visual effects tend to entail 'offended emotion' and 'sensibility confusion'.

If, originally, humanistic thinking is one of the postmodernist aspirations, it has not been successfully transferred to visual form. Resulting from this inadequacy, postmodern graphics lacks the appeal to touch the inner world of the audience in a positive sense (or to commune with the user). In working towards design that communicates, one could learn from this statement: 'For an object or image to have aesthetic or psychological appeals it must first resonate with its audience/user and in general with the society/culture in which it is used or in which it lives' (Dilnot).

But where and how can an object or image acquire these qualities? 'It is the designer who synthesizes a whole range of cultural, psychological and aesthetic factors into the creation of a new object which embodies desires which perhaps the user/audience never even realized they had' (Dilnot). Such a design utopia is a state that postmodern graphics seems hardly to have achieved nor did any other streams of design style did but is there any possibility of improving the situation?

The possibilities of postmodernism
Judging by human-centered design standards, postmodern graphics is substandard: its indifference to human receptivity, a lack of functional simplicity, instability, leaves the reader confused. Yet these missing features are found in modernist ideals – rationality, functionality and clarity although these are also their weaknesses (and boredom).

In chapter one, I mentioned the words of Bauman who 'advocates the acceptance of postmodernism not in the abandon of modern moral concern but in rejection of the typically obsolete way of going about its moral question.'[7] Considering Bauman's concept, and applying in visual communication, one can see it is the inflexibility of modernist graphic design that should be avoided, whereas its basic principles of originality, order and harmony may as well be retained. There must be values in the old system that are just not totally feasible for the new age.

In fact, the emergence of postmodern design style is understandable: the urge to free oneself from any ideological constraints, to seek creativity freedom, self- expression, is nevertheless an act that can be justified especially in the industry of aesthetic production. It is part of man's nature to pursue the new for fun as well as social and economic needs. As Fredric Jameson puts it, 'the aesthetic production today having been integrated into commodity production generally: the frantic economic urgency of producing fresh waves of ever more novel-seeming goods . . . now assigns an increasingly essential structural function and position to aesthetic innovation and experimentation. Such economic necessities then find recognition in the varied kinds of institutional support available for the newer art' (1991, 5).

With institutional support there is always a market to absorb the endless production of kitsch and pastiche. Postmodern graphic design, an aesthetic production, is responding to this economic and cultural development in both Hong Kong and China. For instance, the superficial appropriation of postmodern style in architectural construction is thought (by most mainlanders) to be indicating China's advancement; the stylistic but shocking layout in some local graphic design that has emerged after the trendy approach in Western culture seems to acknowledge our international context.

Due to such economic necessities, postmodern culture is likely to further develop in Hong Kong and China where the biggest market for the variety of design is. I would see the inclination from a critical point of view: given the characteristics of uncertainty, insincerity and pretentiousness in postmodern graphics it might not be an appropriate visual strategy to be used in this very wide context of communication that is young in its design history, peripheral in its design industry.

To pursue a universally-accepted style is impossible but in the context of Hong Kong and China perhaps the integration of different thought styles will be a solution to the crisis of pure postmodernism given the common interests of both regions. By absorbing the essence of the old and the new, a revised model of graphic language may be devised to meet the need.

What we need at the moment is sustainability and practicability as well as the concern for human receptivity – a graphic language that is made accessible (and 'habitable') to people. To work with (or to live with) the postmodern reality we must practice a principled adaptability: an attitude with ethical conception, professionalism, the ability of judgement, in order to produce graphic design of a contemporary look that can be understood and used by our audience, a huge population of 8 hundred millions.

NOTES

1. It is style and function (beauty and utility) that design usually stands for.

2. Karsten Harries, *The Ethical Function of Architecture*, 1997, p. 21.

3. Ibid., p. 8.

4. Debates on modernism and postmodernism in architecture include Jahns words, 'architectural postmodernism represents a realization and a response to modernism [which] produced building without connection to site, place, the human being, and history,' whereas Harries suggests that postmodernism has its origin not so much in a humanistic as in a merely aesthetic response to modernism. Karsten Harries, *The Ethical Function of Architecture*, 1997, pp. 7-8.

5. Clive Dilnot, 'What is Post-modern?' *Art History*, Vol. 9 No. 2 June 1986, p. 245.

6. Ibid.

7. Zygmunt Bauman, *Postmodern Ethics*, 1993, p. 4.

'Habitable' Visual Language:
Old Attitudes in New Structures

'Columnist Rick Poynor wants to read. That's all. But he's finding it difficult these days . . . it appears, style rules – and a good read is getting harder to find'.[1] Poynor's wish, however, is many people's unspoken anxiety in the flood of unintelligible visuals in the contemporary city.

Graphic conditions outlined throughout this book indicate that people's visual experience is overruled by dynamic forces of our time that aggressively reinvent our needs and ideologies. There is a disappearance of certainties in many things we see: we are engulfed in a visual environment made up of fragmented and equivocal statements that are sometimes 'inhabitable' to us.

Graphic design (as other design forms) used to be perceived as something 'that doesn't happen by accident'. Today however, both the creators and users of design are dropping their traditional perception (one with strict demand for rationality, visibility and comprehensibility) in search of a modern attitude to create, and to adapt to the complexities of social and cultural conditions. As a result our degree of acceptance to a greater variety of advertising language and graphic styles did increase. But we are still threatened by advertising manipulation and graphic exploitation.

If manipulation functions with the reader's consent (see chapter 2, p. 63), then my criticism of it may sound invalid. And since the present design phenomenon is an inevitable economic condition, what is the point of my query (and worry) at all?

My goal is not to denounce the present advertising and design mechanism (which is an inevitable and a necessary on-going human activity) but to ask how we can make sense of this existing condition to explore new measures for a sustainable visual culture. In the preceding chapters I tried to rethink technical measures with which to minimize the harmful impact of undesirable graphics. For example, to reorient our attitudes towards design styles, or to review our relationship with the computer.

In this final chapter I should return to a very basic yet significant (and philosophical) question to conclude the book: how can we make the visual culture we already inhabit more 'habitable'? I assume our need for new structures in design by incorporating humanity to the existing mode of addressing the audience is imperative. Humanity is an old quality in design almost forgotten in contemporary thinking and practice but a great force behind the visual power of good graphic design.

To accomplish an 'habitable' visual world requires consensus among corporations and institutions to recognize the importance and value of 'lasting' and 'pleasing' designs in human society. As Manzini puts it, 'it is necessary not just to produce new images but to construct stable and lasting identities that can be placed in a recognizable manner in the cultural space in which we are immersed'.[4]

This can only be achieved by establishing a shared ethos with which designers and related producers (such as printers, contractors), are practically advised and given consent to enforce a controlled and minimized production of indefinite visual commodities (even they can be made with little cost and effort). Ideologically, to produce 'habitable' designs relies mainly on individual designers' conscience and personal values in the act of designing – to acquire an ecology of environment as well as an ecology of mind for their audience.

What then, are the ingredients of such a state of visual communication? And what are their characteristics? Philosophically speaking, a 'habitable' visual world demands works that can function somewhat like a 'thing'[5] or a 'gift'[6] to the receiver – a thing that has 'nearness' to people; a 'gift' that 'satisfies the receiver's needs and desires; that affirms a positive relationship between the giver and the receiver; that makes the receiver the subject of the work and, most significantly, that gives the receiver exactly what he wants without impairing his senses.

Whether a humanistic design is of a prestigious or humble nature, of large or small scale, whether it is an anonymous or professional work, is

野鴿居六號

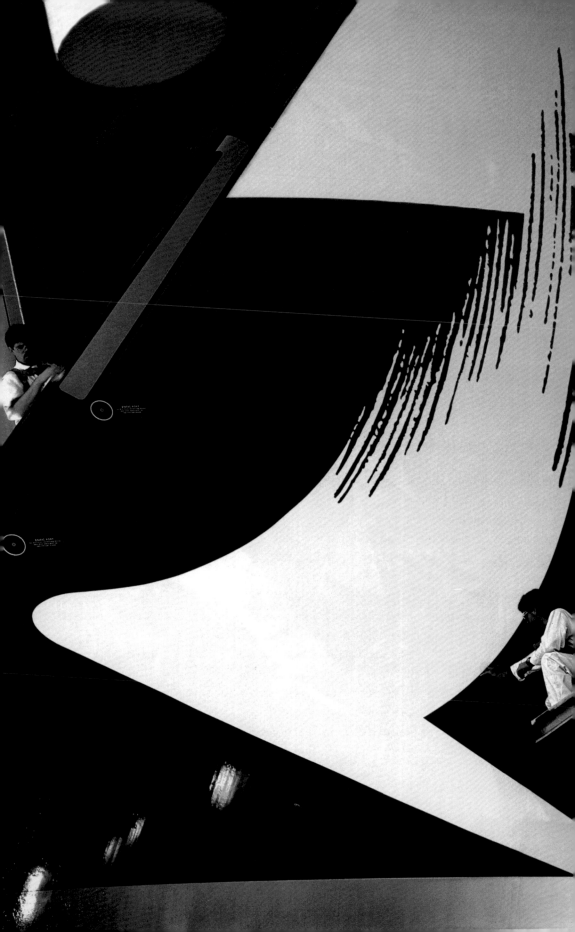

irrelevant. It is its ethical function that matters. A company icon, a simple but intelligible identification that embodies cultural significance, symbolizes the company's business nature and delivers a message to the customer efficaciously, could be 'habitable' to the customer.

Newspaper graphics, simply as a column head, can be meaningful, pleasing and inviting to the reader. The imagery used in the *Hong Kong Economic Journal*'s columns is achieved with the Chinese characters for 'tree' and 'eat'. The motifs resemble the shape of trees and a fish which suitably represent the themes of the columns (writings around nature and environment, food and cuisine). They are both typography and ideography, based on the principles of being easy to read and comprehensible. They are good examples of design literacy.

Image design, being user-friendly and infused with social concern, can be 'habitable' too. I recall that in the 1972 Clean Hong Kong Campaign a cartoon character, the 'Lap Sap Chung' (the Litter Bug), was created to launch the campaign. 'Lap Sap Chung' was presented as a bold, yet interesting humanized character which caught the attention of the then 'unsophisticated public' who could easily grasp the meaning of the message – 'Clean Hong Kong, don't be a Litter Bug'.

What 'Lap Sap Chung' depicted – a villain who litters – was passed on with interest and humor by its strong cultural relevance and its nearness to the public. The purpose of public education was achieved through a positive relationship between the design and the user. The current Clean Hong Kong campaign no longer uses this mascot. Designwise, its appearance may be outdated among more exaggerated animated figures in contemporary advertising promotion. But its spirit lives on as a memorable cultural icon.

In an interview in *Communication Arts*, Kan Tai-keung, a noted Hong Kong designer, was asked how his works managed to attain a high reputation. He said his design attitude came from the tailoring business, where 'everything needs to fit the customer . . . our philosophy here is tailored thinking'.[7] Perhaps the idea of tailored thinking in graphic design should not be directed to a corporation's business objectives only, but to the user's needs by infusing the quality of a gift; to treat the audience as the gift-receiver. This is a new structure in graphic design to which we are looking forward – a visual environment in which our taste, interest, character and preferences are well taken care of, in the presence of visual 'things'.

To pursue the quality of 'thing' one must first identify the limitations of 'object'. Designed objects are basically meant to represent human intelligence, as Frascara points out, 'All objects with which we surround ourselves are a language beyond language, an extension of ourselves, a visualization of the invisible, a self-portrait, a way of introducing ourselves to others, and an essential dimension of humanity' (1995, 26). But today physical objects often misinterpret our needs, as do contemporary visual objects.

Frascara is referring to the physical objects that we possess through the process of selection, that is to say: we choose them to represent ourselves. The major problem with visual objects is: in most circumstances we are the contained (human beings as the spectator, audience, viewer) in a container (the visual environment) in which we are unconsciously and inescapably located. Although we may also choose to read a book, or not to watch TV, on most occasions graphic objects in the visual environment simply exist without having been selected. But they surround us nonetheless.

The unfriendly visual 'object' may transcend to a visual 'thing' when spiritual value is embodied. It is not the physical material (like a paper poster) itself that can become a thing, but the satisfaction generated from the positive interaction between the poster and the viewer, be it a well-delivered message or a meaningful image. It is not an object we hold in our hands, nor an advert we see with the eyes, but a combination of both the form and the matter: the signal it gives to us that is favorable to our senses.

Also, at another level when 'visuality'[8] is present, an 'object' becomes a 'thing' to the user. 'In most cases, the better the design, the more invisible it is', writes Alexander, 'one uses daily objects without seeing or experiencing consciously their design until it comes to using something that is poorly designed'. One may possibly have this experience in one's visual encounter. If so, it is not impossible that visual objects can be spiritually 'invisible'. While invisibility means effectiveness in a mental sense, it is the 'visuality' in the mind of the viewer, rather than the visibility of the object, that is functioning.

We can look at the question of spirituality in a less abstract and more basic way. Victor Papanek mentioned a new aesthetics in design: 'All objects, tools, graphics and dwellings must work towards the need of the end-user on a more basic level than mere appearance, flamboyant gesture, or semiotic statements. Nevertheless, the lack of any spiritual basis for design will make ethical and environmental considerations mere well-intentioned afterthought' (1995, 235).

In Papanek's opinion, a design arrives at an ethical state only when nourished by a deep spiritual concern for people. 'It is the intent of the designer, the intended use, the fulfilled need that can endow even the humblest object with deep spiritual values' (1995, 235).

Take an everyday example like directional signage in an Mass-Transit-Railway (MTR) station – a set of carefully-devised visual forms that has proved to convey meaningful messages to passengers year after year. Since its implementation in the 1980s, the signage has enabled tens of millions of passengers to travel with ease, be they aged illiterate, educated executive or schoolboy, resident or foreigner. Being identifiable and user-friendly, it is the 'visuality' of the sign graphics that is functioning: they are 'things' to the commuter who uses 'internal perception' as well as 'external visibility' to access the information.

A visual 'thing' elevates the user's visual experience because the designer, in the act of designing, has infused ethical thinking to enable ease of use. Spiritual value quite often can be observed in graphics meant to deliver a social and political expression: for its having a keen connection with people extricated from being profit-oriented. In fact fantasy-driven and lavishly-produced designs do not necessarily embody spiritual value. Papanek draws the designers' attention to the claim that, 'if we design with harmony and balance in mind, working for the good of the weaker members of our society, we reform . . .' (1995, 223).

Even a 'humble object' (or trivial low-end artwork, one may say) may demonstrate the designer's ethical concern rather than design

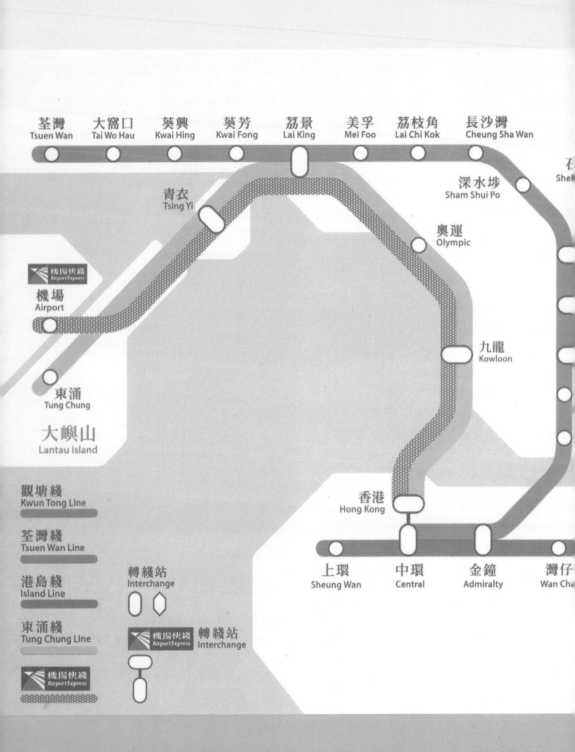

荃灣 Tsuen Wan 　大窩口 Tai Wo Hau 　葵興 Kwai Hing 　葵芳 Kwai Fong 　荔景 Lai King 　美孚 Mei Foo 　荔枝角 Lai Chi Kok 　長沙灣 Cheung Sha Wan

石 Shek

深水埗 Sham Shui Po

青衣 Tsing Yi

奧運 Olympic

機場快綫 Airport Express
機場 Airport

九龍 Kowloon

東涌 Tung Chung

大嶼山 Lantau Island

香港 Hong Kong

觀塘綫 Kwun Tong Line

荃灣綫 Tsuen Wan Line

港島綫 Island Line

上環 Sheung Wan 　中環 Central 　金鐘 Admiralty 　灣仔 Wan Cha

東涌綫 Tung Chung Line

轉綫站 Interchange

機場快綫 Airport Express

機場快綫 Airport Express 轉綫站 Interchange

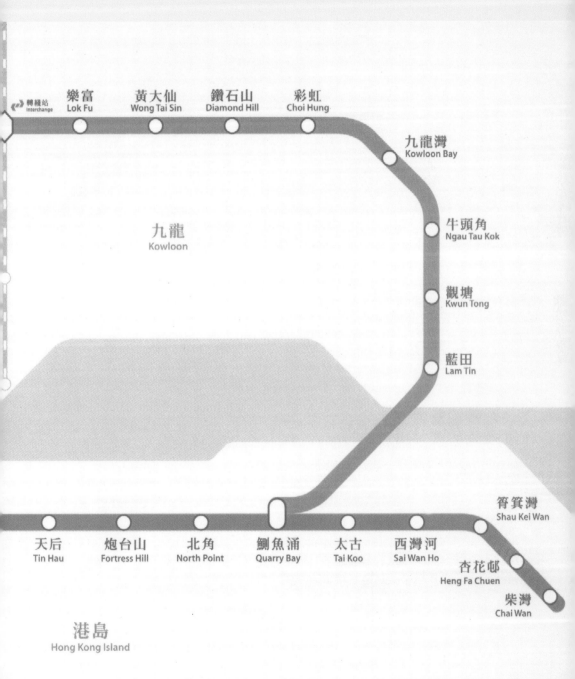

樂富
Lok Fu

黃大仙
Wong Tai Sin

鑽石山
Diamond Hill

彩虹
Choi Hung

九龍灣
Kowloon Bay

牛頭角
Ngau Tau Kok

觀塘
Kwun Tong

藍田
Lam Tin

九龍
Kowloon

箇箕灣
Shau Kei Wan

天后
Tin Hau

炮台山
Fortress Hill

北角
North Point

鰂魚涌
Quarry Bay

太古
Tai Koo

西灣河
Sai Wan Ho

杏花邨
Heng Fa Chuen

柴灣
Chai Wan

港島
Hong Kong Island

pretentiousness. Take, for another example, a series of crudely-printed medical and health pamphlets distributed in a public clinic: the series of 2-colour leaflets was formulated on the basis to help others by means of simple text and clean graphics to explain to laymen measures of disease prevention.

The translation of difficult knowledge into comprehensive illustration helps the less-educated understand otherwise complex medical terms – somewhere the designer can manage to act on a moral basis. The responsible creation of communication products that involves working towards 'life's greatest good' for the readers, is the realization of an ethical thought.

Some may find the above-mentioned designs dull, unimaginative and conservative as they may not fit with the social dynamic of the modern city. True, they are humble generic-looking examples but they happen to retain a 'habitable' quality – what is missing in the mass of communication products that provide no meaningful message just superficial aesthetics. Such inconspicuous quality can be useful in perpetuating good intension in design. So understood, the coexistence and integration of 'habitable' sophistication with radically new, stylistic clarity, are of great necessity today.

For a contemporary designer to return to the conventional attitude of design takes courage because there are opposing forces even from within the design community. In fact, as Poynor puts it, '[people] have poured scorn on the very idea of legibility' (1999). Simplicity and legibility are signs of non-professionalism, even wrong-doing, in the eyes of radical designers and beholders, despite their humanistic value. Thus, this 'rare' perspective – to advocate an 'habitable' visual language – requires a designer's conscience and determination to confront the dominant trend. Even so, maintaining a healthy suspicion of this trend, is a wise thing to do anyway.

As stated at the beginning of this book: this study is just my quest to challenge the optimistic perception of Hong Kong graphic design. My abstract arguments on the undesirabilty of the dominance of superficiality in contemporary graphics, though illustrated with some examples, I understand, are uneasy to be admitted by many practitioners. But the least I can do is to provoke their awareness of the design phenomenon.

A conclusion like this – which suggests a return of the basic goals of design – may bear little convincingness in the current social-cultural climate. Even more so when, after writing this book, I have come to realize that the attitude towards design (of both the creators and users) are somehow changing – from a relatively unconscious disorientation to a deliberate self-indulgence. This adds difficulties to my proposition. For now, I feel it is doubtful whether one can recognize the value of an 'habitable' alternative, or the need for an alternative of a different kind, to the existing visual language.

NOTES

1. *Graphics*, 1999.
2. W. F. Haug, *Critique of Commodity Aesthetics: Appearance, Sexuality, and Advertising in Capitalist Society*, 1983, p. 6.
3. In Manzini's sense, the need for an 'habitable' world comes from the negative impact of technological innovation in the living environment (*Discovering Design*, 1995, p. 222). I see the crisis posed by technology and cultural forces in graphic design has made our visual environment somehow critical to inhabit, that people should contribute to the production of an 'habitable' visual world, a world of stable, pleasing and lasting images.
4. Ibid., p. 223.
5. See note. 3 of introduction chapter, p.38. for an interpretation of the meaning of 'thing' in the design world.
6. Gift-giving is complex in the modern society and the very common 'bad conscience' can be seen in the act. See 'The Gift' by Clive Dilnot, *Design Issues*: Vol IX, No. 2 Spring 1993, p. 51. I borrow the concept of real gift-giving and the meaning of real 'gift' into describing the perfect condition of the work of graphic design which I feel is most essential in building the best design-human relationship.
7. *Communication Arts*, 1998.
8. The term 'visuality' is defined in *Oxford English Dictionary* as 'mental visibility, a mental picture or vision'.

References

Abbas, A., *Hong Kong: Culture and the Politics of Disappearance*. (Hong Kong, Oxford University Press: 1997)

Aldersey-Williams, H., *World Design: Nationalism and Globalism in Design*. (New York: 1992) pp. 8-21; pp. 156-163

Althusser, Louis., 'Ideology and Ideological State Apparatus', *Mapping Ideology*. (London, Verso: 1994)

Alexander, C., Ishikawa, S., Silverstein, M., with Jaconson, M., Fikadahl-King, I. and Angel, M., eds., *A Pattern Language: Towns. Building. Construction*. (New York, Oxford: 1977)

Bayley, S., *Taste: The Secret Meaning of Things*. (USA, Pantheon Books: 1991)

Bauman, Z., *Postmodern Ethics*. (Oxford, Blackwell: 1993)

Berger, J., *Ways of Seeing*. (London, British Broadcasting Corporation and Penguin Books: 1977)

Bierut, M.; Drenttel, W.; Heller, S. & Holland, DK. eds., *Looking Closer: Critical Writings on Graphic Design*. (New York, Allworth Press: 1994)

Bond, M. H., ed., *The Handbook of Chinese Psychology*. (Oxford, Oxford University Press: 1996)

Brody, N.; Brier, D., ed., *Typographic Design No. 2*. (New York, Madison Square: 1994)

Caplan, R., *By Design: Why there are no locks on the bathroom doors in the Hotel Louis XIV and other object lessons*. (New York, Mcgraw-Hill: 1982)

Coopers and Lybrand, *Consultancy Study on Service Exports: Professional and Technical Services draft Final Report*. (Hong Kong, Trade Development Council: 1996) pp. 41-50; 68-74

Crozier, R., *Manufactured Pleasures: Psychological Responses to Design*. (Manchester and New York, Manchester University Press: 1994) pp. 1-45; 78-117.

Dilnot, C., 'The Gift', *Design Issues*. Vol. IX, Number 2 Spring 1993.

Dilnot, C., 'Which Way will the Dragon Turn? Four Scenarios for Design In China over next half century.' 1997.

Daniel, M., *Material Culture and Mass Consumption*. (Blackwell: 1987)

Doordan, D., ed., 'Early Modern Design in Hong Hong,' *Design History: An Anthology*. (Cambridge, MIT Press, 1995) pp. 200-212

Doordan, D., ed., 'Chinese Modern Design: A Retrospective,' *Design History: An Anthology*. (Cambridge, MIT Press, 1995) pp. 213-241

Dormer, P., *Design since 1945*. (London, Thames and Hudson: 1993) pp. 9-21; 91-98

Enright, M., Scott, E., and Dodwell, D., Eds., *The Hong Kong Advantage*. (Hong Kong, Oxford University Press: 1997) pp. 44-77

Frascara, J., *User Centered Graphic Design*. (London, Taylor & Francis: 1995)

Featherstone, M., *Consumer Culture and Postmodernism*. (London, Sage Publication: 1991) pp. 65-111

Goldman, R., 'Advertising and The Production of Commodity-signs', *Reading Ads Socially*. (London, Routledge: 1992) pp. 37-60; pp. 155-176

Harries, K., *The Ethical Function of Architecture*. (Massachusetts, MIT: 1997)

Haug, W. F., *Critique of Commodity Aesthetics: Appearance, Sexuality and Advertising in Capitalist Society*. (Cambridge, Politic: 1986)

Heidegger, M., 'The Age of the World Picture', *The Question Concerning Technology and other Essays*. (New York, Harper and Row: 1977) pp.115-136

Heller, S., Bierut, M., Drenttel, W., and Holland, DK., Eds., *Looking Closer: Critical Writings on Graphic Design*. (New York, Allworth Press: 1994)

Herd, D., 'In Search of Identity', *South China Morning Post*. Nov 3, 1996.

Jones, J.C. *Essays in Design*. (New York, John Wiley & Sons) pp. 6-34

Kinross, R., *Fellow Readers*. (London, Hyphen: 1994)

Kinross, R., *Modern Typography: An Essay in Critical History*. (London,Hyphen: 1992)

Lawrence, R., 'Hong Kong on the Brink', *Print*. March/April 1993, pp. 21-31
Lupton, E., *Mixing Messages*. 1996

Manzini, E., 'Prometheus of the Everyday' in Buchanan, R. and Margolin, V., *Discovering Design: Explorations in Design Studies*. (Chicago: University of Chicago Press) pp. 219-243

McRobbie, A., 'Postmodernism and Popular Culture', 1994, pp.13-23

Norman, D. A., *The Design of Everyday Things*. (New York, Doubleday Currency: 1990)

Papanek, V., *Design for the Real World: Human Ecology and Social Change*. (Chicago, Academy Chicago Publishers: 1992) pp. 59-75

Papanek, V., 'Toward the Spiritual in Design', *The Green-Imperative: Ecology and ethics in design and architecture*. (London, Thames and Hudson: 1995)

Rand, P., *Design Form and Chaos*. (New York, Yale University Press: 1993)

Rand, P., *Thoughts on Design*. (New York, Van Nostrand Reinhold: 1970)

Sparke, P., *An Introduction to Design and Culture in the Twentieth Century*. (London, Routledge: 1986)

S. Berger & Lester, R.K. Ed., *Made by Hong Kong*. (Oxford University Press: 1996)

Tester, K., *The Inhuman Condition*. (London, Routledge: 1995)

Toorn, J. van, 'Thinking the Visual; Essayistic Fragments on Communicative Action', Bauman, O., *'And Justice for All . . .'* (Maastricht, Jan van Eyck Akademie: 1994) pp. 141-150

Turner, M., *Made in Hong Kong: A History of Export Design in Hong Kong*. (Hong Kong, Urban Council: 1990)

Images Credits

Every reasonable effort has been made to acknowledge the ownership of graphic materials included in this volume. However in some instances the copyright holders could not be traced. Any errors will be corrected in subsequent editions provided notification is sent to the publisher.

photo: front endpaper, p. 100, Hong Kong Polytechnic University
p. 10; p. 47, Urban Decay
p. 28, *Ming Pao Weekly*
p. 42, The Optical Centre
p. 96, The Chartered Society of Designers Hong Kong
p. 104, Wiggins Teape (HK) Ltd.
p. 109, CAX2
p. 122; p. 135, *Hong Kong Enterprise*
p. 125 (upper right), Matthew Turner
p. 161, *Hong Kong Economic Journal*
p. 162, Landor Associates
p. 166, Hong Kong Mass Transit Railway Corporation